#1816 was my top producer and the bird that all the "girls" flocked around

Spinner Magazine Worldwide

Copyright © Dave Henderson

All Rights Reserved

3rd Edit

Volume 5/Feb-March 2018

I would like to dedicate this issue of Spinner Magazine to two great roller men I knew who passed away over the past year.

Dominic Carton of Ireland

Dominic was truly an amazing person. He befriended me shortly after I got back into roller in 2013. We had some great discussions usually late at night before I would go to bed along with Eric Laidler of Denmark. There was a lot of discussion moving about and Dom, as I called him, was a real educator above all else with a great sense of humor. He actually wrote several articles to share in Spinner Magazine early on. He assisted me in my major article about the history of the BR in Vol 1. We had a lot in common and he would give me a bad time about being a "Henderson" from Cork, Ireland. These were great talks we had. It's amazing how someone in another country could have similar ideals. He was mentoring his grandson with the birds too, it was great to see. I always wished my kids enjoyed my birds more. He will be greatly missed in this World. I miss you my friend.

Randy Wilson of Savanna, Oklahoma

Randy and I go way back to the mid 1990's. I had gotten acquainted to him of course through the rollers. In those days most of us wrote letters and talked on the phone for the most part. Randy was always a breath of fresh air to me and we hit it off. I talked to Randy last about 2 years ago, as we all know things go fast when you are working and enjoying family life. I sent Randy a nice array of good rollers back in the late 90's and he flew these birds for many years. I met Ferrell Bussing because of Randy and many others in Oklahoma when they invited me out to judge the Oklahoma State Fly. It was great times and I was treated like a king by them. We had some great talks and he was an avid fisherman. I feel kind of empty that I was not able to say bye to him. Randy was a heck of a guy and a true pigeon man and great family man. I feel so bad for his family and he will be greatly missed in life.

IN THIS VOLUME

The Passing of Some True Friends……………………………………………………………………..4

Assessing My Hawk Problems by D. Henderson………………………………………………7

Is it Gone by A. Johnson……………………………………………………………………………….11

What I learned this Year by D. Henderson………………………………………………………15

Competition Rules by D. Henderson………………………………………………………………25

Pretzel Breeding by D. Henderson…………………………………………………………………32

Tri-County Flyers……………………………………………………………………………………………40

Spotlight on Riaan Naude ……………………………………………………………………………..42

Dr. Spintight Q&A…………………………………………………………………………………………..51

The Pensom Legend by D. Henderson…………………………………………………………… 58

The Plan by V. vanRoyen………………………………………………………………………………..65

Ted Mann………………………………………………………………………………………………………70

Editor's Note:

I had to do the cover of this issue over again, bad color scheme. Another mention is early was that I took a conversation with an importer that there never was a ban on birds shipping out of South Africa, but there was for a period of 2-4 year period. The outcome was a more stable importation using the USDA Labs here in the USA to quarantine the birds.

I hope to hear from some readers on what they think. You can leave a review at several sites that would assist me in knowing how you like this and my other issues.

Thanks for your time and have a fantastic 2018 Season.

Please send inquiries to Dave Henderson at davesrollerpigeons@gmail.com

Thinking Outside The Box

Assessing my Hawk Problems – Follow up
By
Dave Henderson

Well it appears my thinking that the recessive reds simply attract more birds of prey is getting to the stages of a reality for me. I will display more evidence of this here in this new update. As noted in my first article about this it is completely counterproductive to breed and fly them here where I live. This really upset me initially because my old line family was primarily recessive red and black for many years and these were amongst my best birds. It's weird how things change over time.

I did some very interesting things in 2017 and in this I ended up having only 7 recessive reds for the entire season. I have been messing with the South African blood lines for the last couple of years and wanted to get a solid idea of the tendencies in them as crosses to my old line of rollers. I was hoping this would help me to get going in a direction with them as crosses and reduce my number of stock birds at the same time.

I didn't produce as many as I would have liked to but I did get the results I was thinking I would see.

I ended up using a total of 19 various combinations of birds, pairs, this past season. I had planned more but ran into a few obstacles along the way with some just not liking each other and refusing to pair up for the most part. I also didn't have any foster pairs to speak of so the numbers were low in terms of a production number per pair only averaging 2.9 babies per pair on average. As most know this is a very low figure and not very productive but having only flew 55 birds here these are the numbers I have to work with.

Again of the 55 I flew only 7 were recessive red, 12.7% of my production. Of these 7 young birds 6 were taking in the first 3 months of life and 4 taken as babies in training. The remaining recessive red hen survived the entire season and developed into a descent pigeon before gifting it to a close friend of mine here getting back into rollers. So on these number that is a nearly 85% loss rate on them even in low numbers.

The greatest thing I noticed was that I actually had 50% less attacks then on past years which yielded more hawk free flying days. I suppose this could have been a fluke, or am I already reaping the benefits of this experiment?

Of the 55 I trained and flew here 19 were taken by the birds of prey, which is actually less than 40% (34.5%) losses on the year. This on its own is a huge wake up call to me when the outcome of my last article was 57% losses over a 2 year average, surviving 20% more birds is literally HUGE. This would be equal to the percentage of losing 31 of the birds produced in 2017 to the BOP this season instead of the 19 I did lose. I will list the significance of this of this equation below.

In 2017 I bred the following colors that were trained and flown; blue/dark check 23, black 13, recessive red 7, red check 7, lavender 2, tort grizzle 1 and 1 blue bar for a total of 55. I didn't not distinguish any white on the birds as I have not really noticed anything significant with white on the birds at this point. I actually bred more birds but had donated them to various things or gave to friends. I can only use the figures of bird that were actually flown out here by me and have accurate numbers based on this data.

I actually lost multiple birds on 4 different occasions that account for 9 of the 19 birds that were eaten.

This cock is a survivor from the 2016 season that become the type of bird you see in 1 out of a 100 birds produced in my opinion from my old line. A 20-30 footer that is an unbelievable who spinner possess the whole package and this henish cock bird couldn't be any better in my opinion.

As you see by 2017 numbers I actually increased dark checks to 41.8% of my birds produced up from 17.6% with a two year average prior to 2017, this is an increase of nearly 25%. As noted this could be all the information I need to see to minimize my losses here. The percentage of losses this year that were blue/dark check was 21% of the dark checks produced and 9% of the total birds produced and flown. This on its own is crazy… When the two year average on the losses of dark checks prior to 2017 was 46% based on how many dark checks I produced. This is less than 50% losses just with dark checks compared to the 2015-16 seasons.

I think in reality I can see an immediate relationship with there being 50% less attacks over a full season. Meaning the hawks came around less than in past years. Had they came by more frequently this year the losses would naturally be higher and considering I only had 1 recessive red remaining they would have just taken whatever they could get I think.

I think the worst situation I have is 80-90% of my losses are with training babies and this hurts the most in reality. I could be losing my best birds before they even learn how to fly and roll. This is maybe the most disheartening aspect of this sport/hobby here in the US.

I have recently have completed an interview with one of our South African counterparts, which you will find in this issue, and has lost only 2 birds to birds of prey in the last 14 years he told me. This in an incredible advantage not only for competition flying but for building the absolute finest family of rollers you can. This allows you to be 100% sure of every bird you use in stock by flying out for at least 2 years before stocking. It gives you a completely different look at birds and how you cull them. Not to mention you actually get to CULL birds…

The way it is now there is not enough birds surviving here to even have to cull them on average, if they are a real cull I would hope the hawks are getting them but I can't be assured that this is the case. The BOP are culling them for us and not the worst birds either but the complete opposite. So the issue is by not knowing it's a crap shoot.

Looking at the other numbers we see based on losses by color;

Recessive reds = 85% losses (7 produced)

Blacks = 46% losses (13 produced)

Blue/Dark Check = 21% losses (23 produced)

Red Check = 14% losses (7 produced)

Lavender = 0 losses (2 produced)

Grizzle = 100% losses (2 produced)

Blue Bar = 0 losses (1 produced)

The big difference this season has been that I actually was able to survive about 10 really good pigeons. Several are very good pigeons that will help me progress my program I feel. In the past I would see these pigeons developing but they never survived to maturity on average. The adult birds' biggest predator would be the area falcons. The biggest predator on training babies is the area Cooper. The Cooper can still get adult birds but most are young cocks that tend to be wanting to pair up at times. They are distracted by things and that end up being their weak link.

If these losses continue like they were this year it won't take more than one season to have a decent team of birds moving forward and then you build on this as you go. So at this point is where I think pumping up the volume a little is my best bet in getting enough good birds.

Let's say I breed 75 kit birds in 2018 and 37% are taken by the BOP, this will yield me 47 birds come this fall, two full kits of birds, even at 40% I would end with 45 birds. If I can't select a decent kit from 2 kits then the pairs just didn't nick like I had hoped but in this case I should be fine considering past results. I just still have to watch my number of recessive reds I fly I think. I am bound to get some every year I breed my birds.

Well again this data here is good information to assist me in moving forward in my own program. I need to find my best pairs and produce as many as I can from these birds. These are high percentage pairs. The odds are tipping in my favor slightly and it doesn't take long before it's a buffet here again so you have to follow protocols. Mine is after each attack you lock down for 3-4 days religiously. This takes discipline but if you do this the BOP are forced to go somewhere else to eat. If possible you also want to change up your fly times at the same time, but this is not always possible with working stiffs like myself.

It's best to fly young birds daily but it's not needed if were are talking about survival. If you fly less it will simply just take them longer to develop.

I hope you all reading have a fantastic season and don't hesitate to email me if you are not fully understanding of the information put forth here.

Here is one of the survivors this season

Featured Article

Is it Gone
by
Aaron Johnson

This bird is the REAL DEAL with Speed/Quality, seen her at 9 years old

What is the Birmingham Roller breed all about, for me it's about speed and high velocity. As long as the bird kits tight and possesses the speed I am striving for it's worth a try in my program. I look for a blurring ball with incredible rapidity in their acrobatic performance as it descends to the ground like a knife cutting through butter.   The bird has to possess the whole package but without extreme velocity it will never made the stock loft.

I have done a lot of traveling with the birds over the years and there appears to be some things that have been forgotten about in many lofts out there, or just simply have not seen what I am referring to in terms of velocity and true spinning. This could also be attributed to the fact that very few now have a true hold over kit these days. It almost appears that many don't have the ability to manage an old bird kit, but it's really hard to know for a sure. I just see many stocking the few good yearlings each season and then getting rid of the rest to make room for the new season. I don't see an issue building up your stock loft with quality birds, but there should reach a point where you don't need to stock birds and can afford to keep birds in your kit boxes, so this is kind of a head scratcher to me.

This Blue hen is superior in Speed/Quality and nice depth

There is no doubt a lot of things at play here from time available to "play' with the birds with a normal busy life style, or possibly the cost of keeping too many pigeons. I just know that there are no short cuts and if you don't put the time in and properly evaluate your birds your progression will be greatly hindered and the more birds you keep can compound this problem. Most areas have the Birds of Prey and this plays a big role in many of the things we used to take for granted for many years. This for the most part is creating a system where we are forced to stock outstanding pigeons before we might have done normally in the past because they might be the key bird to my program, but if I keep flying this great pigeon there is a big risk of it being killed by the BOP.

I really think the lack of a hold over kit has a lot to do with management issues and a lack of experience to handle them. As a result of the lack of experience to fly these adult rollers many are lost due to poor management skills. If you do the math it's all a numbers game but you just never know which bird(s) will be your best ones or things would be a lot easier to build up a stud of true spinners. As a result of this there are many high velocity spinners that showed potential are lost or wasted in the mix. So it leaves most of these fanciers with nothing more than a "scab" kit.

One of my major concerns is thinking that possibly the quality of the competitions we are seeing might have something to do with the rules we are flying with these days. I can't confirm but possibly it could have a direct relationship to the rules we are using. I think this statement says a great deal but I know this is not the only factor that could be at play here. You show me a competition with slack ambiguous and molly coddling rules and I will show you kits that are lacking to some degree or another. I am not at all suggesting that I have the best birds out there but I am just frustrated that things seem to be on a down turn at the moment. Competition rules I feel must be fundamentally sound in that they literally set the standards for guys to breed by. We must have high standards to follow on the World scene. I think that rollers could be one of the hardest breeds to develop to a high standard of performance anyway, so there is really no "free lunch" here.

It's unfortunate but with a heavy onslaught of the BOP with a down swing in the economy has done many things to our current hobby and sport. The entire equation plays a part in what is going on. I find that you have a have a good knowledge of what constitutes a high quality spinner and this does not come easy in some areas. You find quality standards can change from some regions, even using the same rules, so the fundamentals must be an issue here, at least in part.

It's hard to sit here and write what a top quality spinner looks like and it's much easier to show people what they do and how they should act while doing it live and up personal. You can create high quality birds that are able to compete in kit competition but it is not an easy task, especially when erecting a full kit of them. I think a lot of it is social media these days, guys talking up birds when they very well may have never even seen the bird as good as they get in performance but the hot and cold sides of thinking can influence others and do this very easily which is the negative side to social media and the birds, but also the good side at the same time. If people are pushing mediocre pigeons as high quality spinners then there is no wonder the quality has become more mediocre.

If you have been around long enough you will know that top quality spinners that have high velocity are rare and then to have birds that have this and possess the "whole package" are even more rare, so many may not have seen birds of the caliber I am talking about in todays' world. Birds are so easily exchanged these days that it's a total crap shoot. If you realize that all birds are not created equal or up to specific standards I am talking about then if you all up to you do the best with what you have. I think guys that become "collectors" can also affect a lot of what goes on in social media.

We see many chasing pedigrees or lines of birds just because they are popular and this is the wrong approach. Guy are paying hundreds of dollars for unproven birds and expecting miracles out of them. I don't know what to say except that things are going down very fast in my opinion. The quality of the birds are at a low in my opinion. I know that this is a hobby but at some point I was pushed to develop my own breeding program and I guess it's just hard to expect others to see the big picture like I might.

I was fortunate enough to be mentored by some very top quality roller breeders here in Canada and this has left a lasting impression me. Once you have seen the quality I am talking about you will never want anything less. This type of quality is rare and undeniable in every way. I wish everyone could see and know what I know. I guess it's kind of a like a high performance car, once you have winning combination of driver, car and engine design you have to maintain it and at the same times keep looking to better things and refine processes involved with racing this car.

This guy is a real worker and very Tight and Fast

I feel very fortunate to be writing this from what I know and have seen. I have a great perspective on the hobby and have seen a lot of lofts and judged a lot of regions. I know that competition encourages improvements in the breed to the standard they are judged but we have a lot more obstacles these days that are hindering the overall outcome that we experience.   The issue comes when all areas are not equal with these obstacles so you have to work your program around all these facets and at the same time get the most out of your rollers. Some birds just might not cut it in specific areas of the country and this can be part of this as well.

I can only do as much as I can and I will continue to do all I can to leave a longing impression of what a high caliber really is and the qualities they possess. We need to keep these aerial acrobats in the air where they deserve to be.

What I have learned this year
By
Dave Henderson

As many have learned in past issues I have been experimenting with some of the "South African" birds that many have seen and heard about here in the United States that were imported by Ron Swart in 2010 send over by Hannes Rossouw of South Africa. These birds within Ron Swart's own program took off like gang busters for him and in my view of it really didn't miss a beat from what they were doing in South Africa where they came from. This has been very unique compared to many other imports that have taken place here in the US over the years.

I have heard about many of these brought in from places like the UK and for the most part guys are disappointed initially. I think much of this has to do with climate and the birds acclimating to the area where they were imported to. I feel the interesting thing with South Africa is that it's climate is more similar to places here in the western United States in comparison to the UK region that is cool all the time and very coastal type environment. I can't say for certain this is the cause and effect to how Ron Swart didn't miss a beat with these birds after importing them, but it could be.

I think as most know geography and environment does play a huge part in the management for roller guys everywhere and let's not forget the friendly neighborhood "BOPs". What I would give to live in an area where the losses are less than 10%.

So anyway getting back to the heart of this article and what I have learned.

This is the 3rd season I have been able to work with a few of these South African birds, some directly off birds imported, and I really decided that my best approach was to try all the SA birds I had on my own as crosses and see what all the tendencies are that I discover with this philosophy at play. There is a common link with my birds and the SA birds as a "general" sense and this is thru a single hen behind my line that was ½ OD Harris. I did notice right away in a few of the pairs "the goods" in 2017 and moving forward this also gives me a better direction on how to proceed, so in general this was a very successful test, even though I "wasted" a whole season doing it. Some might say well why would want to cross these birds like this? Basically I was initially looking at these SA birds as an outcross to my own line of birds that are very good on their own in respect and thought that the OD Harris side in both lines might have carried over all these years and mix with them successfully. My idea has worked and now am a bit closer to having a real crossed line of these now that really work and in terms of the "pure" lines I also have a better direction.

If you take into account what my initial interest was and what birds did the best I got a solid direction from this with both sides and in order to keep what I move forward with I must have birds that work in harmony with each other and now I am moving towards this.

The biggest downside to this tactic was I was unable to produce a lot of birds from any one combination. I did not create a lot of birds from anyone pair but swapped the pairs around quickly getting only 2 rounds per combination on average. I figured this would give me a good idea of what I had and I would say for the most part it worked.

I have been talking to others that I know that have been working with these South Africans to find out which birds in which combinations are working for them. The ones I know and trust their judgment have given me similar studies but many are just not sure at this stage in their breeding of these birds. One of the biggest complaints I have heard in them is very poor percentages of good spinners on average. Many have their own biases for whatever reason but you simply note what they say and continue to learn on your own thru trial and error.

I have personally seen a link that appears to be a key in the birds I have, even with the crosses. The link I mention is via the Infamous "Stripe Wing Cock" as pictured below here.

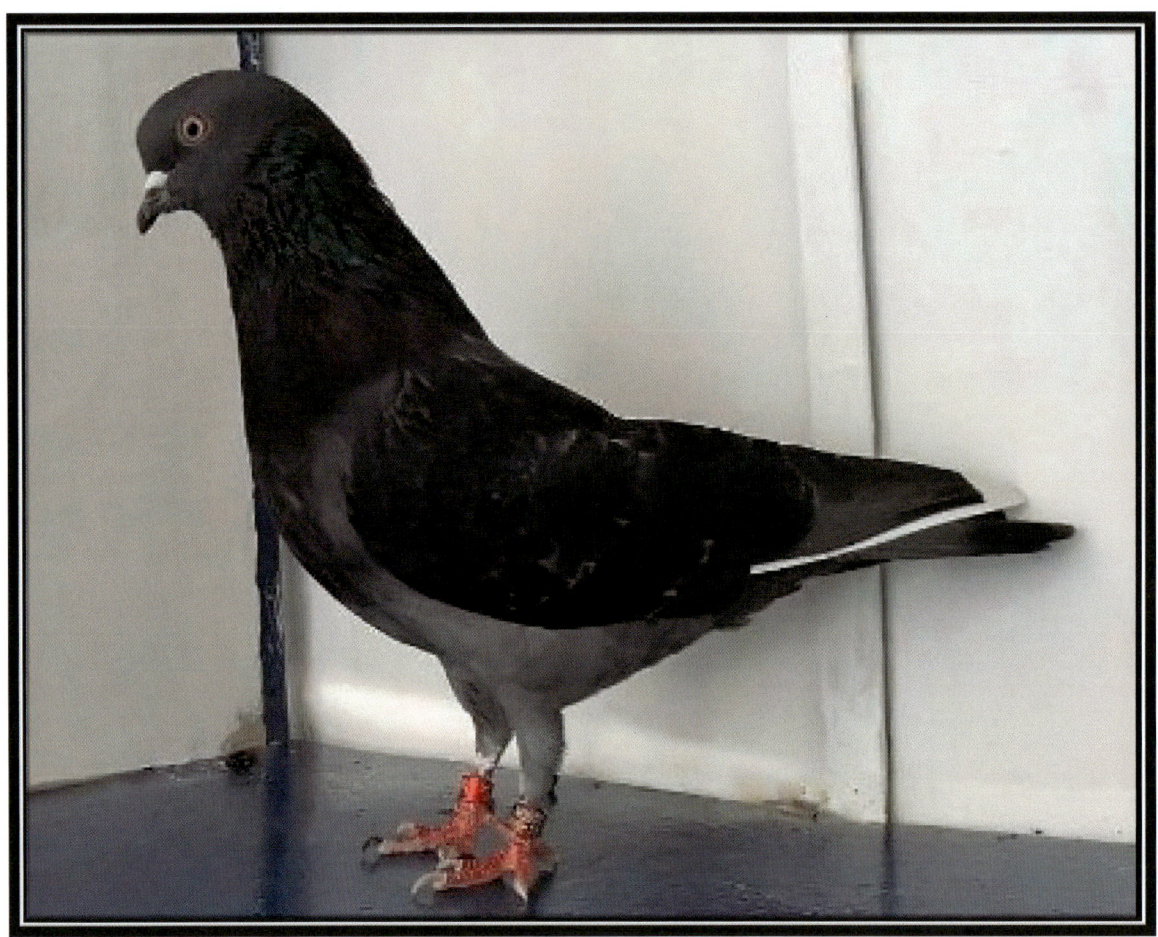

"The Stripe Wing Cock"

#184 JAR 09 Dark Check Stripe Wing bred by Hannes Rossouw

Upon a closer look at #184's pedigree you immediately notice that the dad's side is actually down from Brian McKenzie which is also from South Africa. The bottom of the pedigree is mostly stuff that was bred by Hannes and there is the grandma on the mom side that has a lot of unknowns in here pedigree also, but they appear to be from Hannes' earliest birds that formed this line.

When I asked Hannes about the McKenzie side he told me these were developed by Mckenzie but that he had started McKenzie in rollers in the 1990's with birds he had and his all have similar sources to the Hannes birds. So they are similar in genetics background on them but different enough to create Hybrid Vigor in them when paired together. This meaning mixing the Hannes line to the McKenzie line. Riaan told me that the best kits that he saw flown at Hannes was during the years when he was crossing his to McKenzie's. After future investigation I find that all 3 of these guys mentioned got birds from Jimmy Roodt, now passed, and they had a strong genetic side with OD Harris birds. So Hannes, McKenzie and Riaan all got birds from Jimmy and they also have gotten birds from each other having been part of the same local club for many years, but are no longer close enough to each other for this.

(Please see Riaan's interview also in this issue of Spinner Magazine)

As I know and many others that when specific fanciers get their hands on a line they shape them into their own. This is due to fanciers' not selecting birds exactly the same and over time the birds actually change in type due to this simple fact. There are biases, conscience or not, that some don't even realize they have until they begin to take on the same type. This doesn't happen overnight, 8 or more years or line breeding gives us the biggest change I feel. This is especially prevalent with lofts that refrain from bringing in outside sources of birds. These birds become unique to this specific fancier(s) this is all the good and bad characteristics within these birds.

Looking at many of the pictures at Hannes' loft and birds that he breeds from, his best birds seem to be reds and most are cocks from what I have seen on average. I could only assume that Hannes tends to line breed to the cock side in his line of birds and pushing all his best birds on these particular cocks. Upon interviewing Riaan, who has birds from the same sources behind his birds says his best birds tend to be hens and with this he tends to line breed back to great hens. Those who have breed Hannes birds will know that they seem to produce more cocks then hens on average. I have had pairs give me 7 cocks and 1 hen out of 8 young in a season. I think depending on how the fancier develops his family, their line, that they can affect these things. I myself have developed a family that tends to produce more hens then cocks on average and I have always line bred back to the hens in my line. This could be the difference in these South African birds that have a similar background and the differences in how they were bred.

Another facet I discovered looking over pedigrees and interviewing both Hannes and Riaan is "Inbreeding". Hannes seems to have a more progressive approach and this has him inbreeding more and Riaan not as much inbreeding but more of the "Pretzel" breeding I practice in my own loft. *(Refer to the article in this Issue also)*

Different breeders develop families differently and it's hard to know how things will really evolve until you have been working with their genepool for an extended period of time. It would be like someone buying birds from Pensom's loft directly and then after 10 years of breeding and developing this genepool on their own they change and don't even look the same as they once did. Due to the simple fact with selection these birds change and are never the same as they once were. These birds will basically become your own line based on how you select them over time and there is nothing you can do to prevent this from happening. The interesting thing is that many over a long period of time of say 20 years working with them will continue to call them by the breeder name you originally got them from, like calling birds that are still around today "Pensom's" when we know Bill Pensom died in 1968. It's hard to know why people will do these things when everyone knows they are your own birds now in today's world.

I have seen things in recent years where birds from a well know fancier was at one time calling his birds old line Pensom's and then sometime in the early 2000's started calling them Harris birds, meaning OD Harris. I remember the talk on these 1980 OD Harris imports and many were not happy at all with them, the birds were resold several times after about 5-6 years of possessing them. A lot made note that they produced a lot of roll downs and not living up to the expectations of them at the time. As most know OD Harris also died in the late 1980's if my memory serves me correct. You will find that guys that "sell" birds will shape the birds to the market place to sell more birds, suddenly we see a lot of South African birds available so this is when you really need to pay attention to individuals and not so much on "South African" as a whole. There are good and bad in every family or strain of birds out there.

In the performance world it should really not matter what the genetics are behind them as all lines and families are developed from key individual birds and the influences you see in these birds the same. There is really no advantage for you to just go after birds because someone says they are from a specific line, this is the easiest way to be disappointed in the end. Over time everything you have is what you made them no matter what the genetics are behind them.

I know that there are guys that have birds that claim have never had an outcross in them and all came from a specific source and continue to call them by this source and there is really nothing wrong with this but when you are out trying to sell more birds due to the genetics then this is really false advertising as I see it. Buyers should be aware that just because they were once "Monty Neible birds" does not mean they are now. The birds are from whomever selected them and continued to breed from them over many generations.

As I mentioned above my birds all go back to a single OD Harris hen that was down from a 1980 import that Joe Kiser and Joe Borges did back then, but they are what I made them on my own in today's world, the original hen was bred in 1985. When looking at the genetics on the specific birds I developed in the line from they are approximately 40-50% OD Harris from this original hen that I line bred with. As you begin to line breed them tighter and tighter over generations it's your aim to get them more like specific birds in your own loft not bred to birds just because they have OD Harris blood in them. Guy that breed birds based on lineage (pedigrees) will mostly being going the wrong direction unless they are very familiar with the line in question and how to use a bird but for someone to sell a high dollar bird based on its pedigree alone is the wrong approach in my view in the betterment of the hobby. This type of stuff leads to guys making up stuff just to sell birds in the end and the buyer needs to be aware of this fact. The paper is only as good as the reputation of the person that sold it to you...

The particular bird in mine with OD Harris blood in it came via Chan Grover in 1988. Those who knew Chan knew he was really a "collector". He enjoyed having a good array of birds from all the popular lines and this never changed as long as I knew him. After a while they were known as "Dave Henderson birds" and were what I had made them and when I advertise them I do not label them as "OD Harris birds" or even "Bradford birds" as that is also part of them. I think that when you begin to do experimental crossing of birds it's all very uncertain territory on how they will evolve over time but if you are selecting by the same methods you select everything by they will stay true to your selection processes and the crosses will have to do what you demand of all your birds. They will change to the characteristics you are looking for which encouraged you to do the outcross in the first place, but they will change to some degree or another with every cross you do.

Getting back to these South African birds.

I know the Stripe Wing Cock is still alive and producing birds, but I have never had the pleasure to have the Stripe Wing cock in my loft first hand so I really don't know how he would have evolved at my own loft. But as I go thru the best birds I have that have SA blood in them all of these birds have a common link to the **Stripe Wing Cock** to differing degrees including my best crosses.

The best birds I have produced have all had the Stripe Wing cock close in them. I wondered if he might be the key to this entire shipment from South Africa. I have talked to a few I know that have been working with these South Africa birds over the last several years and all that are getting descent results that have the Stripe Wing cock directly related their program to some degree or another, but as noted the percentages are not as good as they like on average.

I know several that also have had some great results from birds directly related to the "Badge Pair" (215/220). I personally prefer birds that are super high velocity even if in the 20 foot range over the slower birds in the 30+ range. So this might give you an idea of what I am looking for.

Having had many of the SA blood here in my loft some are larger and bigger chested birds and others are more "pipie" in their type similar to my old line of birds. I have done so little breeding with the "pure" stuff that I can't really give a definitive break down of specific bloodlines in the shipment from Hannes and how they are working overall. I too am kind of a progressive type and in this you have to get thru the birds as fast as you can to a specific result you are looking for, meaning the birds will leave quickly if the results are not definitive enough to keep them. When you put pairs down in several combinations and start to see a pattern then this should give you direction to move towards. It takes good record keeping to find it faster. If you pay attention you will see what is working and can start to consolidate your flock to the birds you like the most. I can only hope that I have kept the birds that will continue to progress my genepool for many years.

As I see it even if the pure lines of the SA birds don't work I have already developed very good cross lines with my old family of rollers that I know is working and I am on my 3rd generation with them. So if anything fails I have my old line and the crossed line I can concentrate on just like many others do with competition birds with high velocity. To me it's best to find the birds that are actually working and work them as quickly as possible. Birds that aren't working you have to give a limit on when to move them out or you will become a collector like many others. I would say if you have not found a key mating in about 3 seasons it's time to move it out. It does not matter if you paid big bucks for the bird you have to move it out.

One I bred that is fantastic, ¾ SW genetically

I have seen mixed body types in these South African birds from Hannes, some are a bit larger and bigger chests, some are short but have larger chests and then you have the slimmer body birds that I prefer as these seems to be the fastest birds, same as they are in my old lines of birds. Granted after stocking the birds they do put on weight and will change in body type slightly due to being locked down and lacking the exercise they used to get.

The South African birds I have used tend to be early rollers, but this would be birds between 5-7 month mature spinners. I have heard of some being closer to a year old before they have a mature deep spin but even in my own birds I don't stock any bird that is later than 10 months developing into a mature spinner.

This above picture of the stripe wing cock is while he was still flying in the kit just before he was shipped to the US. So he is in shape and not like your normal bird that has been stocked up for a while. He is more filled out these days and was more thin build in his prime.

It has been my own experience with my old line of birds that the greatest influences come from "henish" cocks in terms of performance with speed/quality. What I know of my old line is that the best cocks tend to be a shorter (depth) spinner on average and a slight decrease in performance in comparison to my best hens. The game changer comes in the cocks that looks like a hen and have the performance of the best hens, this makes for a very special cock bird in my opinion.
I have handled these SA birds a lot and the cocks have larger vents on average too which is also characteristic to the henish cocks. So it is possible that his best cocks started out similar to type as the hens with these SA imports?

I know a big thing I notice in the SA birds as compared to my own or even the crosses with mine is that many of them don't have fast reactive type pupils that many talk about. It's odd as many have said over the years that the fast adjusting pupil that goes from very small pin point to larger very quickly is a quality many have looked for. However in these SA birds this is not the case, at least with many I have looked at in my own loft. I can't really say for sure in birds still residing in SA as I would have to visit to assess this.

I have heard and several have confirmed to me that the birds that possess the darker brownish colored eye, walnut color many call them, also tend to be the most dangerous birds. This means birds that bump things and can roll down even, but like anything I am sure there are exceptions to this. Hannes recently asked me how some of the import pairs produced and what the birds from them did. I told him the 184 (SW cock) and 108 produced some good spinners and many, especially the hens, were a little too hot on average and even produced some birds like this. **He replied in the image below.** My friend Tim has confirmed this to me and Riaan also confirmed this to me with the brownish eyes, especially in the red checks. These two tend to have less of the darker eyes and more of the normal pearl type eye. So I am left with thinking that you can't really assume anything either way but just work the birds you like and develop them into the spinners they can become.

Many over the years I have talked to that flew good spinners will confirm that if you have a good spinning family that you are going to get some roll downs and bumpers and like Hannes references here you need to learn how to handle these birds so as to get the most out of them. I think one aspect that many of us here in the US have is the heavy BOP issues and with this makes it very hard to keep flying good pigeons over and over each season to get a better assessment on their long term tendencies and get the best stable high velocity spinners you can get in to your stock loft.

I wish I would have witnessed the creation of these birds that Hannes made in the early days and how he selected them, this would have been an interesting process to see firsthand and you gain more knowledge on his processes, however like all things there are several ways to "skin a cat" and these refer to the steps to get to the desired destination. I know after communicating with Hannes many times over the last year or two that his program is very progressive and has a lot of inbreeding in them. He will not hesitate to raise a bird fly and breed out of it at 6 months of age if it can speed him along as all go back out and continue to fly anyway. Would you think that maybe Hannes is doing some intense inbreeding? I have no idea really as its specific birds with specific plans in his loft. I know what I do in my opinion a lot of inbreeding is not really needed, it just speeds up a process that will force you to outcross quicker if you do a lot of inbreeding. Intense inbreeding will cause a lot of issues but some swear by it, I suppose it could be something that you can do with specific pigeons and it doesn't work with others but it's just my view that it's not really needed at all with cousin lines. I think it's the blood in the SW cock that is the Game Changer here if you ask me personally if you are after speed. He mixes well with several of the other birds in the shipment and I am not that only one to notice this.

A little known fact is that there was a hen imported from Hannes and she was #108/70 JAR 09 that only lived 1 season after arriving. I am not sure what caused its sudden end after getting to the US, but she left a solid impact when paired to the SW cock, #184. There are a handful of cocks off this pair around and all seem to be very pre-potent to producing good fast spinners, and some good speed and depth in some. I had heard that many of the hens for whatever reason were on the deep side or would become roll downs, these daughters also can produce the same so as a pair it might not have been the best combination, but the cocks seem to be super stars. Just like everything they are not all the same and you could get some exceptional deep stable hens and cocks. One of the better known hens from this pair was a dark check hen #271 that Ron stocked and was simply known as *"The 5 Second Hen"*. I have been lucky enough to get ahold of some of the grandkids off the pair and they are so far so good in my opinion. It's especially nice with my BOP issues that these are more of the blue pigeons that have a better survival rate here where I fly.

#108 JAR 209 Red Check Hen

I think that the key to creating success is by having ½ siblings and 1st cousins and working them together. I think it only takes one successful combination to kick start your own program and its taking the kids off this pair and pairing them to other related birds to see if it sparks something to move forward with. It's all trial and error but if you get it to work then you are on your way and make sure to pay attention to this. You could inner bred a small family like this for a long time without doing a lot of intense inbreeding.

One complaint I have heard often with these South African birds is that the percentages are just not as good as they like. They see good birds but few and far between. I know some of these are good breeders and flyers I trust but others not so much, so it's hard to pin it down and explain this on average. I think a lot need to produce more birds from pairs to test them more, you HAVE to use a scientific approach of you are just "farting in the wind". The more you breed them the better idea about what are "YOUR" best birds in your specific genepool and this will give you the direction in which to go. If you don't keep good records you will never find the direction needed to progress these birds, so much of this goes back on the breeder at hand. This simple thought needs to sink in, "All birds are not good producers no matter how much you paid for them…" It takes effort on the individual to make anything work, it's not something that happens automatically it takes time and a lot of quality time paying attention to the birds on hand. I suspect that many that have these birds will just need to line breed to the SW cock to get going in the right direction, but in today's world where many have no pedigrees or knowledge of background will have to resort to the all trial and error method but if you are persistent you will get there in time.

If you see guys crossing a lot of these birds it could be that they are having issues developing them together "PURE" and instead of just canning them you experiment by crossing them to something you are more confident with, another strain or family. This type of behavior is very common and as noted I have done a bit of it myself. I have not however canning the line in hand just experimenting. Had I not had only one South African cock in the first season I might have done it in the beginning but I did so it's only obvious I would have to pair this bird to a hen and had no SA hens available.

We know that Hannes was very progressive with these birds and often breeding from birds that were bred in the same year even. It's due to the lack of a lot of BOP in this area and this can allow you to find the very best stable birds. I know many wish they had this same situation, I know I am one of them.

I know a few that are making strides with these birds and the key, like anything else, is working a small gene pool and line breeding to these key birds the key birds are not the same with every genepool and they might not be closely related even. I think a major issue is that most just keep too many pigeons to give the "key" birds justice and at the same time are losing key birds that could take them to the next level or their pairs are just not producing enough babies to fully evaluate your pairs. A very unfortunate thing is that most of the original imports have now died and much of what could have been done is now gone such as the #108 hen. As time moves along we only have what we have to work and need to move forward in your endeavor.

All I can say at this point is I feel much more confident this year in the stock I am using related to these imports and I think they will assist my program moving forward, but it is all still in the early stages to say I have a "gold mine" here with them. I am sure there will be some obstacles but I think the key is just working with fewer birds that are related and trying to harness some of the qualities in these that fit my program and management practices. After all if these did not handle the same as my regular family of rollers I would not be wasting my time with them. I am not suggesting they are not showing me something I think will help me because is not true at all, I am very confident that what I have will give me what I am looking for moving forward in all facets.

As many know time restraints hold many of us back and we are only able to do what time will allow us to and this is a big part of what I am referring to here. If I was retired fully and could fly more birds then I currently do and had little risk of losing them I would be progressing at a faster rate I feel, but being the "working stiff" I am things move a little slower but they do progress non the less.

I know one thing for certain and that is that some of the crosses I have developed are exceptional pigeons in any loft and after 3 seasons of working them and seeing how they are progressing I feel very good about what I have going with these crosses I have developed. This year, like every, will be another season to test my ideas on them.

As some have seen or heard I have a pretty severe BOP problem here where I fly and it seems to be linked to specific colors I am flying here. The recessive reds being the greatest attacked and eaten. The BOP are relentless when they see these colors in my kits and continue to attack until they get one, but when I am not flying any birds this color the BOP don't tend to come around as much. I am lucky that the crosses of these SA with mine line creates more standard dark checks and red checks than anything else, so this on its own lends to less attacks. After testing this theory this past season I actually have 50% less attacks on the adult birds then I did in all previous seasons going back to 2014.

Well I hope you all gain some insight in this article and I will continue to update my readers with my progress with these birds.

There was a ban on the importation of birds coming from South Africa shortly after Ron got the birds. It was due to a bird flu strain they had in SA. Breeders tried many facets to get their birds out of South Africa to no avail and many good birds being destroyed in the process at times during that period of time. The ban was lifted and bringing the birds in to the US was streamlined but the process was more expensive and it will be possible but with more fees in place to do it then before.

Hope you have a great 2018 season.

The Birmingham Roller
A Performance Pigeon
A 2014 Published book

New Book available at amazon.com/Hardback version at LULU.com - search by author

★★★★★ Great book for the novice, rookie, and veteran.
By Brandon Hendrickson on December 26, 2014

After having rollers as a boy and now being the new guy to the hobby once again, I gained a lot of information from Dave's book. He gives a lot of good tips from the basics of building your kit box and loft(s), obtaining birds of good quality and how to approach a fancier on the matter, to breeding birds and even eye sign. I found his chapter on night flying very interesting. And in today's day and age I really found the internet links to be very helpful as well. I will put a lot of the information in this book to good use and reference back to it through out my experience with these beautiful birds. I recommend getting this book if you are a beginner such as myself, or even a veteran. I am sure you will find some useful tips to add to your arsenal. It is new age with up to date information coming from a man with many years of experience in the hobby of BR.

★★★★★ Birmingham roller a performance breed
By Judith Crespo on May 11, 2014

This book is a great source of information. It covers all topics from understanding the roller pigeon, acquiring your stock, to creating your own family of roller pigeons. I really enjoyed learning more about roller pigeons from an expert like Dave, who is a superb representative of what the sport is really about. Thank you for sharing your expertise with all of us who care about the roller pigeon sport/hobby. I would definitely recommend this book to everyone who is interested in the roller pigeon sport/hobby.

Ralph Crespo
Belleville, NJ

Edited Revision out February 2015, more pics, few new chapters etc… "A common sense approach to breeding and flying the Birmingham Roller as a sporting pigeon. Good practical advice for all levels of knowledge. Illustrated throughout, this is essential reading for anyone interested in learning about this amazing performance flying pigeon."

Dave Henderson - davesrollerpigeons@gmail.com

Competition Rules – Get better
By
Dave Henderson

The rules in place for the current World Cup and NBRC NCF events need a little fine tuning to their rules on scoring our rollers. There has been a lot of things brought up over the years and one of the earliest I recall was judging the birds within a ½ second of the first bird breaking. This over time was deemed inferior and I would have to agree with this change.

There has been other adjustments made all in the efforts to create a competition that is fair for everyone to follow and that includes the judges doing the scoring.

I recently did a survey with several World Cup judges that agreed to answer some simple questions about their experience judging the World Cup. I think like all judges they are trying to do the best they can while still keeping to a specific standard in the competition. The biggest issue is the rule in place that states "**8) Integrity. The judge shall NOT score anything that does not meet his standard for adequate quality and depth or duration of performance. This competition is for ROLLERS and not tumblers! Roller flying is a subjective sport and the judge may have to make allowances for extraordinary circumstances. In any case, the judge's decision is final and anyone verbally or physically attacking the judge will be disqualified from the fly and may be banned from future WC events by the WC committee."**

The rule that is shown here in quotes has created a lot of headaches in my days of flying in the World Cup Fly. The rules give a definition for "adequate" and clear language but this rule allows the judge to essentially disregard the rules entirely and select and score the kits as they see fit. I can see the reasoning behind it but there also should be a rule that states the judge should follow to rules as closely as possible or keep the field of competitors aware of what will be scored by all judges the judge the event. I might also suggest that if a judge does not follow the rules as they are written that specific judges should outline how they will judge and submit this list of what they will score and what they expect to see in the kits that will be judged in the finals. This list should be forwarded to every fly region and even posted on the World Cup Fly official website for others to view at least 30 days before the finals event starts. I really don't think that this is too much to ask for as to minimize confusion and give an expectation to the competitors.

I would like to thank Joe Emberton, Ferrell Bussing, Eric Laidler and John Wanless for participating in this survey. I invited several others but they didn't see the relevance of the questions I set forth or did not reply back in time to make this article. Either way I appreciate the participation and this gives me an idea of things, I mean we did get two from the US and two from across the pond so it's at least fair numbers. I realize that not all the questions are in reference to this particular article but I thought if I am doing this might as well get some other information that I could use later on with other topics in this regard and added more questions no really relevant to this exact topic. I had no intentions of publishing specific fanciers' answers with their names attached just to get the thinking behind them and relate this to the others surveyed as well as my own experiences.

I think there has been a little confusion about how to award the bonus multipliers as well as calling out breaks. The rules clearly state that waterfall is not to be scored, "**at least 5 must ROLL together in order to score.**" This rule used to say "**roll with within ½ second of the first bird breaking to score a break.**" I think this is an upgrade to the rules for sure, however there are some issues about when to score the 5 birds that are breaking together. Does this allow for the judge to judge any group of 5 birds that rolls together whenever you see this so long as they perform at the same time, or does the kit have to fly and act a specific way before you call the 5 birds that are breaking? I see no mention of this detail as it only says **"at least 5 birds must ROLL together."**

Ferrell Bussing Judging the Finals in our Region

I have heard all over the years and but specifically judges not awarding breaks like this at times when there is in fact a group of 5 or more rolling together but the judge hinders the kit due to the kit not setting up properly in his opinion. Seems some want the kits to break, regroup and then break again and not the kits that constantly have groups of 5 or more breaking continuously and yet the birds are not "OUT" because they are rolling and coming back to what is there of the kit so to speak. I have personally judged kits like this and it's a real nightmare on the judge with the constant breaking and I personally might judge several breaks in this series but the kit at some point is unable to control this frequency and constant fury of breaking almost uncontrollable I will at some point stop scoring them until they settle down. Unfortunately I didn't ask this specific question but all said they judged as closely to the rules as they could in their opinion.

I think this rule might need addressing or at least the judge will need to send a clarification letter outlining what they will expect from the said kits when the contest starts. This I find clears up a lot of issues to the finalist in regard to the scoring as it puts everything out in the open prior to the release of the kit. I think this outline should cover everything the judge is expecting to see from depth range to the quality of the spin. It might also give an example of what could happen should the kit be hit by a BOP. Nothing is really out of line in putting in to this outline of expectations.

I think another rule that might need to be looked at is the time flown. I know many in some areas what to fly just at dusk, in low light conditions. Some listed that there should be no birds released within one hour of dusk. This is mostly due to poor lighting when looking at the quality of the birds scoring. Low light is hard on some and I think the finalist should ask the judge what he thinks in this aspect so the participant is judged more fairly. I think this could possibly be part of the judges' outline to the flyers on what their expectations are. I would highly suggest that there is something that will encourage the judges to outline what their expectations for the fly so that no one is left wondering what will happen when they show up. You can't assume anything really but it's should be on the judge to express these feelings prior to showing up. The judge should never assume that a specific region would know how he does things as this sport is so subjective that nothing is the same from area to area for the most part except for how they score the birds.

Many areas might have slightly accepted quality standards then other areas but are not aware of this because they have never been to this area to see firsthand. In a sport like Kit Competition seeing is everything. The system really needs a video made of several different type of kits showing just breaks or a series of break to educate judges on expectations.

Getting into this topic comes the idea of better educating our judges with how to judge the kits in question. This could involve online courses of getting an idea of what to look for and not to look for. I know one thing with video is that it tends to give the appearance of the birds being slower then they might look in reality or "sloppier" then they might look when seeing them at a split second. Only one surveyed was against educational videos to help with the judges' ability to know what he is looking at in the video. This individual felt that these videos would not make the judges all see things the same. I personally know it won't do this, but the idea is seeing other things not just the breaking of the birds to look at.

I think much of this needs to be discussed in live under a real kit and in an open forum. I think specific parts of video of kits that were really judged with a judge(s) under a live kit should be recorded and the score(s) given told to the viewers. In fact they could do this portion with a panel of judges so that you can see what this panel all saw with specific breaks and what they noticed of the kit in question when scoring them. Some guys might have a hard time multi-tasking on the kit, out birds or birds' coming down early etc... and need another set of eyes to watch for this stuff. We know that there is never going to be absolute fair system in seeing birds break especially when they get into larger breaks of over 10 birds. It all takes place within a split second and the really only thing to do with large breaks is look for the birds not displaying a roll good enough to be scored whether due to simple tumbling or just not deep enough in the judges' opinion. I personally think that no properly put together educational videos should be disregarded entirely and there is something good to be seen with everything. After all we continue to learn as human beings for the better parts of our lives so you can't assume this won't help some.

So looking at this the majority of the judges surveyed agreed that some education is needed to better educate judges everywhere. We all know that no one will see everything same but it's is kind of like driving and when some guys nearly cuts you off on the road. It's how you react in that split second that can save your life. This is not the same thing but these are actions that happen in a split second. It's a trained reflex for judges. All people don't display the same physical and mental prowess but you can get better at things with practice. Again this is like no one is every totally correct all the time, it's human error and with something as subjective as judging a kit it will never be without its flaws.

Getting into the middle of awarding bonus multipliers is delicate work. This part is so subjective and depending on when the best kits start in the contest will set the standard for the entire event.

I think the majority of the experienced judges need to leave room for better kits later in the contest and this might be hard if the best kit flown was the first kit flown. All the judges seemed aware of this phenomenon in the contest.

A huge issue I feel is "Quality" inside the kit. This is a very GREY area in the rules. I mean what does Quality mean to the judges that are doing this? Is it how the kit flies and acts? Is it the quality of the birds that are scoring the breaks? Is it

Velocity of the birds scoring? I mean this could mean many things to different judges. The judges really had mixed opinions on this one.

The rule is very vague here and they read as follow; **"a quality factor of 1.0 for "adequate" to 2.0 for "truly phenomenal" based upon the judges overall impression of the average quality exhibited in all the turns scored."** To me it's plain English that it states the overall impression of the average quality exhibited in the turns scored, this mean based on every score you saw the average quality of the birds within that turn scored. So it is ONLY based on the birds that are performing not the average of the birds in the kit. Some think that there should be a specific number of birds in the kit that display the average quality you award and not the average quality of the birds that are scoring all the points.   To me this is a serious issue in the scoring of our kits.

I mean there are obvious things that would discount any kit and the first thing that comes to mind is flying tool high or too far away. This has nothing to do with how they perform in the kit it's just that the judge is unable to see the quality of the birds breaking even if he can see the number of birds that are breaking in the kit and even seeing the depth of these birds breaking in the kit. So if you can't see the quality then you can't score it is easy to note here. However if they are close enough for you to know they are displaying "adequate" quality and depth then they should be scored I feel. So this distance will not be the same for all judges. Again this is a thing that judge should send out to the regions participating so they are aware of what will and will not be scored. Something like this is a simple fix to appease the participants.

I have heard that some participants were told that they did not get a higher quality multiplier because the kit did not perform enough breaks or that they didn't have enough birds with high quality to get the multiplier that only a few have. I have heard some told that their birds were not deep enough to get a higher multiplier for quality. The list goes on and on for this stuff and there is really nothing listed that would discount quality multipliers for a kit based on anything except for the birds that are scoring the breaks on the score sheet plain and simple however this is happening over and over, especially with overseas judges. I am not pointing to our judges that were surveyed necessarily but just a general reference here from things I have heard.

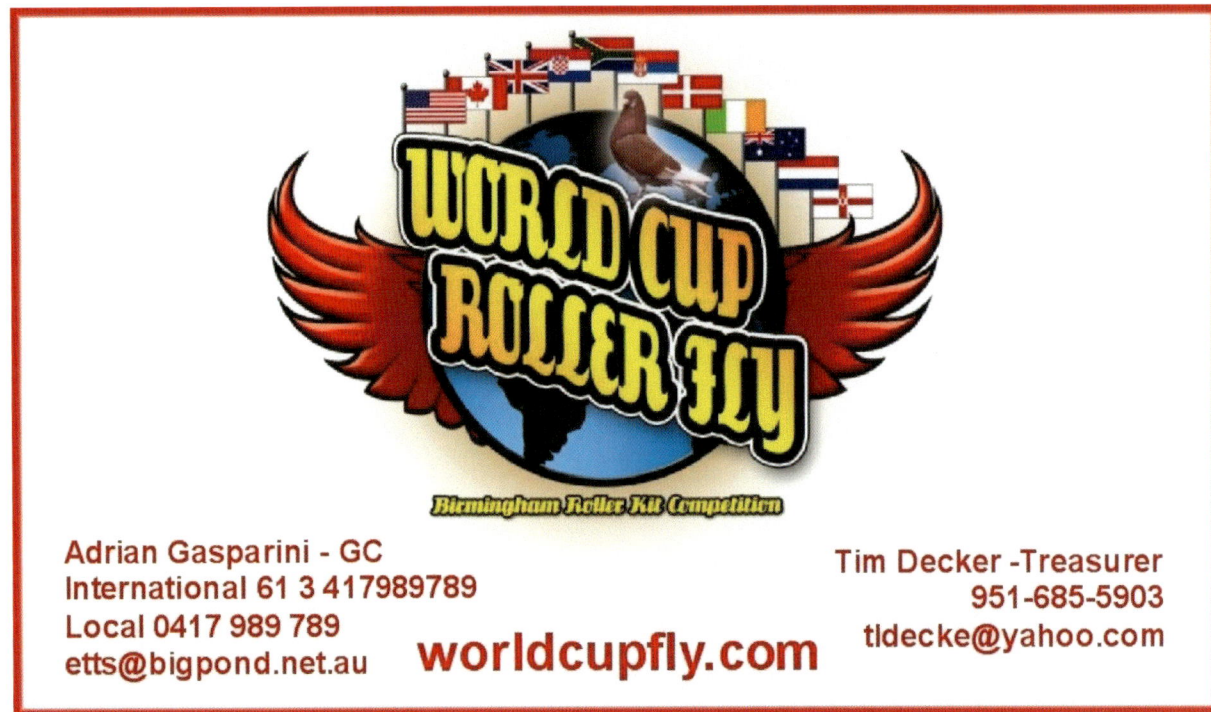

To me personally the only excuse I see above that makes any sense that is listed above is the not enough quality birds to in the kit to earn more quality points. Adequate depth and high quality don't translate the same so this to me is not an excuse but some think that quality is something to do with depth when it's really nothing to do with depth but might have something to do with duration of spin.

I am not totally sure on how they score their kits in these areas of the world but it's obviously not by the same set of rules that were designed and because of Rule #8 they are able to get away with it and explaining away why the 5 perfect rollers in a persons' kit did not receive a 2.0 in Quality for a particular contest when they read the rules and it states **"the overall impression of average quality in all the turns scored."**

I see two fixes for this issue that come to mind here that can fix or assist this particular issue once and for all and stop the frustration in these contests everywhere.

I think personally that awarding a 2.0 is certainly not attainable as the scoring currently is by averaging the quality of the birds in the kit after you judge this kit, however it can happen with another system regularly when this is earned. I can see why this multiplier is misused often and it is as simple as it's written in the rules **"the judges overall impression of the average quality."**

This wording tends to give the impression of the average quality of the kit. The **"average"** could also be based on the average in relationship to the kit being flown. **Example;** if the judge feels that there is only 6 quality birds in this kit then you can do simple math here, 6 birds is approximately 30% of a 20 bird kit, so you can in a way prorate the quality of the break. Say you think that all of 6 birds are 1.8 in terms of individual quality and if you factor out 30% of that it's 54% of 1.8 or about half which means you give them a 1.45 or 1.5 but the rules are not really designed like this as it says clearly **"average quality exhibited in all the turns scored."** This part that you over looked in the above paragraph clearly says all the turns scored, or in other words the quality of the birds that were scoring all the points. If it gave the impression you would discount quality of the birds scoring I think there would be clarification of this in the rules somewhere but there is not.

A simple fix for this is just awarding quality and depth multipliers for EACH scoring TURN that is seen. This would take in account the average from break to break individually and not confuse the judge what so ever. I brought up this issue many years back, 2001 actually, and then revisited this issue in around 2015 when I discovered this topic in some old articles I had been working on, some dating back to the mid 1990's.

This disadvantage to this new scoring is a slightly larger score sheet but it can easily be done with very little adjustments to the judges that are scoring now. You could simply call out the break let's say he calls out an **8** and then followed with **5/5** right after that would be **"Q/D"** and then continue this through the entire fly. Then you simply know it's an 8 bird break and that you multiply 8 by 1.5 and 1.5 which would give that specific break a total score of 18 and so on throughout the event. It would take much longer to add up the score but it would be much more accurate than the current system is. In fact this method would have no real average like with the current system at all. It's a real time score that is given, not an average. Assuming you see a break that would warrant a 2.0 in quality and say a 1.8 in depth you would just record 2.0/8 as displayed. The scoring area of the score sheet would need to slightly larger should with essentially 3 digits per break.

This simple change in scoring would virtually create a dead on system and one where you can't misconstrue what quality means at the end of the event. Not to mention that it could be possible for a judge to outright manipulate the score after seeing the raw score after the fact. I am sure this has happened at times for whatever reason but this would also eliminate that from happening.

Another possible fix, I would not favor this over the first but it can help fix this issue, would be having Quality, Depth and Velocity in the multipliers for bonus. I don't feel that Quality and Velocity would warrant a 2.0 in each category but more appropriately a 1.5 in Quality and 1.5 in Velocity. You can easily range each of these with 1.0 as average and 1.5 as phenomenal in both. The Depth range would still need to stay at a 2.0 based on what we are seeing in kits and gives a greater range of depths within the 2.0 scale that can better award points to the flyer in depth.

As noted scoring would stay the same with the exception on the new Velocity/Speed Multiplier added and range within the scale as suggested. This would completely remove speed out of the quality factor altogether and it would be specifically for quality of spin, wing position as most look for which spinning. Again this is a very subjective part of judging but there could easily be 1.5's in Velocity more often which is appropriate if you ask me.

The one downside with this type of change is that the scores will be inflated more than they are now, but most would not care about having higher scores on average I feel.

Example; let's say last years winner using this new system had 332 raw score and was given a 1.4 in Quality, 1.7 in Depth and 1.4 in Velocity/Speed the score would be the follow, 332 x 1.4 x 1.7 x 1.4 for a grand total of **1106.22**. The difference being the current system might have shown this score, 332 x 1.6 x 1.7 for a grand total of **903.04** points which is an increase of about 20%. I don't think a lot of guys would mind higher scores for their birds not doing anymore then they are now, but with this system is still skewed to some degree in comparison to the first method outlined but will do a fantastic job and clarify to judges more about what the multipliers are to be used for.

I know change is hard for some guys and it's easy to just keep things the same but there is a misconception on these Qualtiy multiplier that needs to be fixed. I think either method will help to even things out a bit as the same time clearing up a misconception of Qualtiy as it is currently being scored. Sometimes it's just minor adjustments that need to happen and this might be the perfect fix for today's premier event.

There was a recent change that made it so you can fly the same kit twice and World Cup only wants the very best kits to advance to the finals so this appeases that to a degree I suppose but I know for most regions it's not going to be reasonable to do two competitions so that everyone has two chances with their A team. This single change took the "crime" out of this from when some in a specific region in Southern California were admitting this had been going on and going on for many years. Granted many I personally talked to in that region were not aware this was going on and did not want to be included in these rumors that everyone in the region was doing it. So instead of penalizing these regions they simply took the crime out of this behavior and at the same time made it so it's no longer needed to fly 2 separate kits for a regions to maximize their flyers going on to the finals. So initially it was needed that every region have as many qualifiers as possible and this meant entering a second kit by all that flew to manipulate the numbers so to speak. I think reducing the number need to qualify is an important step in keeping this thing going.

I personally don't agree with letting guys fly the same kit twice they are outlined in the rules now in some places they can easily do this but others not so much. This will be a region to region decision which is what promotes the hobby more and if things appear like most are getting screwed over then they have the ability to abandon this "region" and start their own fly which is also like a "Self-Policing" action as well. Having rules that force changes is not the right direction and this is something the NBRC is dealing with now in regard to the NBRC NCF each fall. We all have to remember that above all else this is a hobby and one that we are supposed to enjoy not one that causes more stress on us.

Here is the current World Cup Fly rules for you all to view;

1) Kit size. The kit size may range from 15 to 20 birds, but at least 5 must ROLL together in order to score.

2) Time-in. The flyer shall announce to the judge the number of birds that are being flown prior to release of the birds. No additions or subtractions are allowed after release, but the flyer is allowed to chase up any

birds that land or hit before time is called in. If the number of birds released is different from the number of birds declared to the judge the kit shall be disqualified. The flyer has up to 5 minutes after release in which to declare time-in. If the flyer does not call start or time-in earlier, scoring begins automatically five minutes after release. Any interference with the kit after time-in may lead to disqualification. Attempts to ward off birds of prey are allowed, but any directly related kit activity shall not be scored.

3) Fly time. The kit is in judgement for 20 minutes after time-in or until the second bird lands, whichever occurs first. However, the kit shall be disqualified if more than one bird fails to fly for at least 15 minutes after time-in unless driven down by a bird of prey or extreme weather. A kit that is forced down by a bird of prey before the 15 minute mark will not be disqualified and its score will stand. A bird down that spontaneously crashes (after one bird has landed) shall be given up to 10 seconds to resurrect and resume flight or else it shall be considered the second bird down.

4) Time-out. The judge may call a single discretionary time-out for up to 5 minutes in case of an attack by a bird of prey , blow-away, or other whim of nature or act of God, the flyer must ask for the "time-out" and ask the judge to put them back on the clock if he deems necessary before the 5 minute deadline. Although the 20-minute time for judgment shall be extended by such a time-out, the 15 minute minimum qualification time is not affected.

5) Bird-out. Except for a 15 bird kit, scoring shall continue if one bird leaves the kit. Scoring is suspended but timing continues if 2 or more birds are out. A bird is not considered out if it is returning directly from a roll or it has been separated by extreme weather or chased off by a bird of prey - even if the pigeon lands or is captured.

6) Extra birds. If additional Rollers join the kit, a simple discount for the extra birds shall be made for each turn involved. For example, if 2 extra indistinguishable birds are in the kit and 7 roll together, the judge would record 5.

7) Scoring. It is mandatory for the region to furnish a timekeeper/scribe for the fly-off judge for each finalist. The judge shall simply estimate and record the number of birds rolling adequately in unison for each break involving 5 or more. The suggested minimum depth for scoring is 10 feet. Afterwards, the judge shall multiply those numbers by 1 for 5-9, 2 for 10-14, 3 for 15-19 and 5 for 20. Those results shall be added together to produce a raw score. Next the raw score shall be multiplied by a quality factor of 1.0 for "adequate" to 2.0 for "truly phenomenal" based upon the judges overall impression of the average quality exhibited in all the turns scored. Likewise, a depth or duration factor of 1.0 to 2.0 shall be multiplied to produce a final score. The judge shall announce the final score before leaving.

8) Integrity. The judge shall NOT score anything that does not meet his standard for adequate quality and depth or duration of performance. This competition is for ROLLERS and not tumblers! Roller flying is a subjective sport and the judge may have to make allowances for extraordinary circumstances. In any case, the judge's decision is final and anyone verbally or physically attacking the judge will be disqualified from the fly and may be banned from future WC events by the WC committee.

A Scientific Method

Pretzel Breeding
By
Dave Henderson

Some might be wondering what I am talking about here. I never really called it "Pretzel" breeding early on but more just called it "Breeding Lines" or "Cousin Breeding" of related birds and developing separate lines within a line of Birmingham Rollers. The circles make sense here due to how the process works as the basic principle is to create several lines that you line breed to, but are still related to each other. You have the birds you line breed too and then the rest of your stock birds you work into them. It's a very progressive system meaning all but the birds you concentrate on are moved out fairly quickly and replaced by kids or others related to them usually but not necessarily. Much of this again matter on how much time you have on your hands.

When I outlined my breeding concept to my old friend, Russ, he told me I was "Pretzel Breeding" as he had followed my techniques over the years. This is really developing "Cousin" lines from a small gene pool and then mixing them across specific lines and then back to their own line the following year. At times even the birds that formed the line are moved out for a better producing model that is directly related; like a son or daughter or even grand kid.

If you try to reference the term anywhere you won't find the term as such and it's more about cousin breeding with the use of aunts and uncles mixed in and sometimes grandma. By using this method you are not having or even needing to do much inbreeding as the years pass by with a system like this. If you do it right when you do mix the lines at specific points they will generate their own type of hybrid vigor that occurs in a real crosses and that is why you do this method.

For me personally this system started when I did an initial cross and then took the best son off that mating and bred him back to his mother. So early in this process there is a little inbreeding going on with to the foundation birds you start with to help set the type in them. I read this system many years earlier, actually in a 1960s racing pigeon book, and remembered this years later. The literature stated that in the early stages type played a big role in selection, as similar to the foundation type as possible while still being a top performer. The idea is to develop the lines mostly from the hens' side, in the beginning, that has a natural tendency to be dominate in a pairing, especially in type. Having a foundation hen meant breeding birds that are like her. It works best when you have siblings to your "foundation" bird also and ½ siblings. The pairs that will get your attention are the high percentage pairs and then mixing these with others directly related. You can develop a solid program starting small like this and using these in a "Pretzel Program".

When you have the ideal specimen, either a cock or hen for foundation, you will begin by finding a top quality bird off of this bird(s) and pair it back to its parent it outlined a hen in the original article I read. When you make this combination you want, make sure the birds are the cream of the crop, only the best performers. It is very important at this early stage to not cut corner and use a mediocre pigeon in the equation. The old saying is "Garbage in Garbage out." It really doesn't matter which side (sex) you develop but you must keep good records and breed with a scientific method. This means keep track of what pairs produce what babies, how birds develop when flown and if any are roll downs or sloppy and even lazy or hard to manage. I also keep track when the BOP eat them as this could play into the equation also, survival instincts. This might take 2-3 years of swapping pairs around each year and breeding a good number of babies to evaluate them properly, but I would suggest you go with NO more than 8 pairs of birds so you can get thru them quickly, and quickly means 5 or less years. If you are unable to obtain something that is worthy of stocking from this great pigeon you can simply go get another bird(s) and pick them out of the air and pair it to your ideal foundation bird or depending on it you could start over with better conditions that is the great thing with this you can do whatever you want to so long as you are striving for top performance. It's important to have to get birds that can be fed and handled the same. In some families the cocks might be better spinners on average but in most lofts it's the hens that are the superior performers on average.

Sometimes it's just the particular mating that created the high percentages or it could also be a particular bird in that mating that is "Prepotent" and will probably produce good birds on many other good birds you pair it up to. In most cases if you dig dipper you will discover that it is in fact a specific pigeon that has the ability to produce good birds off nearly every pigeon you pair it up to. It's not 100% and really nothing is but this gives you a specific genetic make-up that can be passed along to others as you continue to breed these pigeons in their family lines.

The key is "type" in this system pay a great deal of attention to the birds and their qualities. Speed and style I would personally say trumps depth and this is the direction I have chosen to go in. There are many hidden traits in our birds and some of it is we have or haven't seen but you have to stick to a specific type that is specific in the originals to get the type of bird you are after "set" in them. The originals are the birds are you trying to breed more like so keep this in mind. I am talking about looks, size and of course how they act the high quality spin has to be in all that you take so don't get hasty and try loading up your stock loft with mediocre pigeons early when it's a specific type you are looking for. You can see at times larger birds in the line that might also be a good rollers but when sticking to a program "type" you need to refrain from this for a few years until you get a better idea of what you are doing with them. If you are patient they will come.

Many will say if you breed for only the best spinners that fit your needs then "type" will take care of itself. However it's been my experience that this works to a point but not when first starting out a line especially if they were developed from a cross. As you begin to line breed these birds the "Type" will indeed take care of itself.

You will find hens are of a specific type and cocks are a specific type in most lines of birds that are considered a "family", then this person has already helped you along a bit so to speak, but not always. Some have been doing birds a very long time and in most lofts guys will experiment on the side quite a bit but this does not mean a lot as experienced guys will only keep the birds that they feel can help them in someway. It's simply a way of trying to get yet even better birds. As I see it once you get going you are constantly striving for better and higher percentages of spinners in your program that fit the role you are looking for. With these new experimental versions you must put them thru extensive testing before they are ever considered for stock or at least they should be as they are not considered "sound" until you do so. If they are you could easily screw up a good thing you have going if you jump to the gun too quickly with them.

There is really no issue unless you are so high on these birds that you discard the foundation that made them altogether and then if you find out several years down the road that you made a horrible mistake by putting all your "eggs in one basket." This is not the best approach when you have been working with a solid family of birds for a long time, you slowly discard them as you begin to gain confidence in the near birds but it's never advised to get rid of one for the other before you know what you have. This is why Pretzel Breeding is a very beneficial system as you are really never without the best birds in your program and discarding your program prematurely is not a wise thing to do unless you have seen some so much better than you have it's worth the risk.

You might saw well how do I start to get my Pretzel Program going?

Imagine putting down your original birds on a list and then trying to mix them back and forth until you find the very best combination, something that surpasses all other combinations if you loft? These the birds we are looking for to work with. The key is keeping your program small enough that it's not going to take many years to evaluate what you have, I would suggest 8 pairs or less. The main thing is banding the birds and keep very good records of the babies and the performance of the babies. I would also suggest swapping the pairs around after about 3 rounds with the first mating and then finish up the season with the second mating. My own objective here is looking for the best spinners that also are your best kit performance birds. They don't have to be super deep just high velocity with a quality spin.

Here's how your early program might look while you still have your Foundation Stock and the ring in the middle would depict this foundation bird

Here is your basic Pretzel design, each ring depicting one part of your Cousin Line

There are limitations to all things and your goals need to be realistic, especially when first starting. Let's say a realistic goal is having 8 pairs and raising 40-50 babies and from these number being able to identify survive 3-4+ good spinners that are top notch in quality and speed. Birds that stay tight to the kit are best and the birds that fly out a lot and perform even good spins are not going to help you. Good birds have a drive to stay in the kit and perform in the kit and weak minded birds are the ones you see flying out of the kit all the time.

You have to watch your kit birds very closely to see all their characteristics and how they react in the kit and how they handle the spin when it develops. Many get scared of the roll when they first hit a high velocity deep spin and this is what causes them to fly but birds that are already sexed and start to fly out like this might give you a good idea of just what they are and as I noted this is a major flaw for any performing roller, flying out of the kit often.

These small character "flaws" in birds are easily weeded out but you have to be willing to cull a bird like this even if it is good deep spinner. You have to be very selective of the qualities the birds you might consider breeding from and display especially while flying. There might even be another series of culling in the stock loft due to what is seen in the air, this is a normal progression. I would usually give specific birds about 3 seasons with various mates before I discard them. You are looking for pigeons that possess the TOTAL PACKAGE so you need to find pigeons that are as close to this as possible. If you were to select a bird that is not the whole package the only thing I would compromise on is depth. So if your ideal pigeon is 30-40 foot and you have not good quality birds in this range that are able to do it all then pick something a bit shorter that does.

In my opinion the very best birds are ones you are not even sure of their sex until they are locked up a while as when they are in the kit they are a "kit" bird and kit birds have to do their job as a kit bird does. Their No 1 priority is flying and rolling in the kit at all times. So whatever you have to do to get birds that are like this you do it so that you will eventually get to a situation where the birds doing what you desire of them, a majority of the time. If birds don't do what you want you cull them and stick to the birds that do all the things you want.

As we look back at the 3 circles that interlace posted in this article this is your basic "Pretzel" design as I used to reference "Circle Breeding" years ago. Some might look at this and say "I can't understand this?"

Well I am here to tell you that it's quite simple as long as you line breed to specific bird in each ring or circle. This bird would be the type that is extra ordinary or could be from some extra ordinary parents. When you start to rotate all your birds on all the opposite sex birds you are bound to identify good spinner and if you are lucky you will find a "click" pair in your loft. I would suggest getting several sets of full or half siblings that can better assist you in creating cousins early on. This 3 ring design would say 3 lines that are related, you can expand on this to more rings too, and this would be for each family of birds you have as well, if you have time to develop multiple families for birds. This would be like "sub" family related to the birds in each ring. It would be like adding a small ring attached to the bigger ring.

The thing about this system like I said is it's very progressive and you could easily end up replacing the original "line" bird with its own sibling in as little as 2-3 years breeding seasons. As you see in the over lapping rings where they cross this gives you the range of what line to mix them with and it's with these cousin crossings that you aim to produce a future "line" bird of its' own and then put it back to its' original line the following season. I would guess that about every 2-3 years you will be crossing it over to another cousin line with the hopes of creating a solid spinner in that mating before going back into its line again. You can also keep grandparents around and if they are solid in your program take a bird that is 3 generations ahead of them and then go back to grandma. Like I said not a lot of inbreeding unless you have your original foundation birds intact still.

It's not a complicated program but you have to know what you are doing so you are able to keep them somewhat separate on their own so when you mix them you create "Hybrid Vigor." Hybrid Vigor happens when you mix 2 different line bred families together, it's a way to intensify the genes in the birds and possibly create birds better than both lines individually.

I have created some pairs in this system that gave me incredible high percentage pairs where you can get 7-8 birds out of 10 that are stock quality spinners. It's with these type of pairs you keep the system going on and you can select several key birds from a mating like this and create these "sub lines" to the others. Depending on age and other factors you will ended up down to less "cousin lines" again after several years and then start to process all over again.

You can also simultaneously run two pure lines like this and also keep a crossed line as well and all use these cousin lines in each strain or line of birds.

As I stated once you select a specific bird to do with this you are all in and if it appears to not be working you toss in another bird in there. These cousin lines could even be 3 full siblings or 4 even using a four ring system. I doesn't change you just want to make a list show the pigeons that form the specific cousins you line breed too and then the supporting pigeons that can be mixed to all 3+ lines to assist the program. This is how you can even bring a cross in.

You would bring a cross in as a supporting pigeon to the normal cousins and I would prefer to use a hen but a cock will also work. Your idea with this is to bring in a bird that is showing you something that you are not seeing in your own birds, could be depth, maybe even something like color but it's also displaying all the qualities you are looking for in all your other pigeons.

When you bring in a pigeon like this it's best to be very aware of the family and it's characteristics with feeding and handling techniques so that it might be compatible with your own family. There is no use to bring in a bird if you are not able to feed and handle exactly like your own as this would create more work for you in the end and most likely would end in disappointment. So when you do this be very selective and whenever possible it's best to pick the bird from the air. It might be best to bring in young birds to fly out so you can see this first hand.

A 4 ring "Pretzel" system means having 4 key pairs each season that you feel will push you to the next level with your family and with a 4 cousin system 1 key bird to each of the cousin line birds. The other pairs you use are part time fosters to these 4 but still worthy of breeding from. This was what I was meaning when specific birds can be moved out by other birds as you can get some very good pairs in these secondary pairs this is why you really can't afford to put all your "eggs in one basket."

Each ring of a "Pretzel" system as noted is for one key pigeon I you program and how you bred it within this ring. As the rings cross over other rings you cross over the appropriate bird in that other ring to introduce, before taking anything produced from this mating back to its appropriate line. You might breed 2-3 years before you breed out.

You just can't afford to put all your efforts in one "click" pair and putting a ring on them and stop trying to progress the line. My opinion is if you found one of these key pairs then there will be others. The birds eventually get old or they could even die very suddenly leaving you in a real predicament. Once you ID a "click pair" you need to move each bird around on other key birds to see if you can find a common link, meaning find out if it's the cock or hen's influence or just the combination of the two that made a click pair. When you run cousin lines you can do this by going back to the closest relatives you still have in your stock loft or you can even plan ahead with your hypothesis with other pairs moving forward that will create mates for these others that can further test this.

This is one reason pedigrees are important in a family to the guy who is creating the birds. He is able to see how they were bred and see the relationship of the pairs you are using. This tells a guy a lot when you created the entire line. If you are well versed on your lines background you have some unique abilities and that is creating future stock birds that can be tested without ever flying them. This is not a common thing but with specific circumstances it is. These circumstances could be specific stock bird getting old or you think it's at risk of not living as long as you like. As said above if you a specific type after sometime raising these birds will standout to you. These characteristics are very subtle but if you know what you are looking at you can see it every time it pops up even after coming out of the nest. I don't advise these methods to anyone who is not aware of these things in their own line of birds. Guys can get lucky at times and luck can also take you a long ways if you know how to work with it.

I hope that you are able to better understand what is termed as "Pretzel Breeding" and I hope I didn't leave out any important steps in here. The way you work the "Pretzel" is not the same in each loft, it just gives you a map of when you could do somethings but the road is laid by you as you see it live and up close.

One major advantage to this type of system is that you will eventually get more than you need of top quality spinners and it's at this point you start to move some of these great pigeons to a loft that is open to doing things like you are and you will be able to set them up with maybe another "Pretzel" system at this loft that you can feed off of should you need to sometime down the road. You will be very surprised how this can benefit you getting a quality "cousin" that was bred and selected at another loft. So long as you trust this fancier and that it was not crossed or anything it will be a great advantage to you down the road.

There are a lot of guys that are quality minded and are looking to befriend other good people and this is the way we need to build relationships in this hobby. We work together and we can all reap the benefits of it.

Best of luck to you this season.

Western Canadian Roller Club
Representing British Columbia and Alberta

For more information
Aaron Johnson - aaronspinners@yahoo.ca
Tony Hatoum - tonyhatoum@yahoo.ca or
call 403-808-7438

Deep Spin with Unison

HAWAII PERFORMING ROLLER CLUB
Established 1999

Kulia I Ka Nu'u
"Strive for the Highest"

PRESIDENT
ROBERT PERRY
sugarmilllofts@aol.com
808-349-4813

TREASURER
WALT ROSEHILL
wrosehill@hotmail.com
808-261-3762

WEBSITE
bigislerollers.wix.com/hprc

DA Henderson Roller Lofts
"A High Velocity Tight Kitting Family"

Breeding for to Ultimate Kit Performance Rollers
Old Line Henderson and South African Bloodlines

Dave Henderson - davesrollerpigeons@gmail.com

Inquiries a Pleasure

Available birds are very limited

Welcome; Tri-County Flyers
By
Dave Henderson

I am excited to be introducing the Tri-County Flyers flying roller club here in Northern California, what is known to most as "Superior California." This is just mostly in reference to the beautiful surrounding up this way. The area is about 1 hour in all directions from some prime time outdoor activities.

I started flying rollers in 1980 with the Northern California Roller Club (NCRC) as a Jr member.

A lot has changed in this area since then and high in participation in this area is pretty much linked to a founder of the NCRC, Rex Clark from Orland. Rex passed away in 2006. I had known Rex for most of my life with pigeons and he was a real promotor. He got them early in the 4H program in this area.

After his passing the area really took a dive for the worst and when I gave up my rollers shortly after Rex passed away in the 2007 winter when I moved. My hiatus lasted until 2013 when I would get my birds back that fall prior to the 2014 breeding season.

I tried to reach out to some I knew during that time that were active in the rollers and many were nearly impossible to reach. A few I did find were just more or less out of it with no intentions of being active because they would barely return my calls. After a little investigative work I discovered after Rex died the entire NCRC club pretty much found itself in Sacramento. I had lost track of this when I had been in the Hi Five Roller Flyers up until my hiatus.

A few I did locate were more than eager to get something going which was Ronnie White or Red Bluff and John Henderson of Roseville, who were also part of the NCRC.

Since 2014 it has taken a bit to get things going but I think we are now in a place where it can really take off but we have to really pay attention to our environment so things can operate efficiently for all of us involved.

It is really fortunate that the area is starting to take off as there is another roller club already formed her that has 4 or more members and now with the TCF we are starting out with 5 and set out boundaries in a triangle shape and this is where the Tri in Tri-County came from. The fly area basically covers an area between Redding and Chico which will give us a lot of growth potential. We also have another larger group forming to our south that is being driven by the North Roller Guys out of Oroville, but this area will spread to West Sacramento in the coming season.

Recently a past president of the NCRC also got back into birds, Paul Fullerton, and this is also good news as he is eager to get back flying again. Sacramento had been slowly dying as well since Paul got out of rollers so it's perfect timing to get things going again in this part of Northern California. I can envision there being three real flying regions here now in the near future which will no doubt get other things moving.

We have already talked about having potential "Grudge Match" flies against our neighboring fly clubs.

Well I just want to introduce the founders of the New Tri-County Flyers; Vince van Royen our Club Coordinator, Ronnie White our Treasurer and webmaster, Paul Mabie and James Byrom which are fly members both in Chico and of course yours truly as Fly Director.

We have already scheduled the 2018 season with our Annual BBQ Fund Raiser and three club flies. I think things are really looking up and getting exciting.

Our club BBQ Fund Raiser will be held on April 7th, 2018 rain or shine at Vince van Royen's home, due to his very spacious covered area, here in Redding and there will be a load of great raffle items and quality birds.

If anyone is interested in learning more about the TCF and our up-coming members' functions we have great website put together by Ronnie White that will allow anyone that wants to be an "Associate Member" so you can have access to our club news and other activities by registering.

It's our aim to rebuild this area to its great status it once had and with the numerous clubs that are in play it will maximize efficiency while at the same time being able to pick up others in the area that might want to participate.

For more information please contact our Club Coordinator, Vince van Royen, via our fantastic website at www.tricountyrollers.com

May you all have a fantastic 2018 Season.

In The Spotlight

Interviews in the hobby

The latest issue of Spinner Magazine has it's interview from a South African fancier named Riaan Naude. I have really enjoyed communicating with Riaan over the last several months of so and he has a good knowledge of the sport in South Africa. I recall seeing some pics of the birds a year or two ago calling his birds "Devils Ear Rollers" and have seen this in some birds even here locally at times but that common. It's hard to know exactly why some display these "ears" and others do not. I am sure speed could be part of it but also balance I am sure.

I really appreciate Riaan sharing himself with us and his ideals and practices. I hope you get some good insight from his interview and I appreciate him doing it for us.

Riaan in front of his loft holding one of his prized Devils Ear

Name, age, where do you live; describe your location in South Africa and include your weather climate

Riaan Naude I am 47 and live in Alberton which is in Gauteng South Africa and just South of Johannesburg. The weather is pretty nice here and we get all year long it is mostly sunny or partially sunny here. There can be afternoon showers here as well. Where I live the wind is very minimal. I also have no real birds of prey issues here having lost only 2 birds in the last 16 years.

When did you starting raising pigeons in South Africa?

I started raising pigeons, fantails, in South Africa at around 10 years old. I did a bred Boerboel Dogs for while then ended up going back to pigeons in the late 1990's when I volunteered to clean Jimmy Roodt's lofts for him once per week. I got serious about the Birmingham Rollers around 2001 with birds from Jimmy.

How long have you been working with your current family of rollers and what various families of birds or bloodlines are behind them? Have you ever imported any birds to South Africa?

The family I work with is mostly Ollie Harris (75%) and Ken White (25%). These birds have done very well for me over the last 16 years. These birds are related to Hannes Rossouw's birds he imported in to the USA back in 2010. These birds come from Jimmy Roodt who came in second place in the World Cup. Brian McKenzie, Hannes Rossouw and Buks Knoetze all got birds from Jimmy and have all done well at times in the World Cup Fly. Since about 2008 I have been experimenting with the 4277 Mason line here for competition purposes.

The OD Harris birds that Jimmy had were directly imported by Gert du Plessis in 1971. These are the birds that started these fine pigeons.

To date I have not imported any birds from outside of South Africa

Jimmy Roodt and Heine Bijker

I have seen some old articles that talked about competition in SA going back to the early 1970's, are there any roller guys from that era that are still flying today in SA? Or were when you first started competing yourself?

Steve Naude and Ben Van Heerden we active flying rollers back in the 1970's. They are all still active in kit competition here in South Africa. Steve Naude is a past winner of the World Cup

How did you get started in your current family of the BR and how many pigeons are behind this family you have? Do you have a partner behind the scenes that you work with in conjunction with your breeding program?

Jimmy Roodt got me in to the birds, I used to clean his lofts on Saturdays and he used to give me his feeder eggs. I use to carry the eggs in my under pants to keep them warm on the way home "lol", and then place under my birds. I breed off one hen and her offspring that I got from Jimmy like this

What are your normal breeding practices? Do you line breed or inbreed mostly? Can you describe the type of pairs you like to use in your breeding program?

I breed from Half Brother-Sister, Mother-Son and Farther-Daughter and tend to line breed back to the blue hens. It is the best combinations for competition birds in my opinion. I don't practice a lot of close inbreeding

Who or whom would you say has contributed the most to the CURRENT competitions going on in SA today?

Sparks Axel, Poen Shabodien, Riaan Kruger, Steve Naude, Edgar Roscoe and Nicky Deysel.

Have you ever participated in the Anglo African Fly? How many times has this fly taken place and what are the records for wins that SA has versa the UK? Why is this fly called the Anglo African Fly?

Yes I have participated in the past and it takes place every two years here. I was selected as having the best individual bird in this competition when Johnny Conradie and John Wanless judged it.

We have done this fly 5 times and England has 3 wins and South Africa has 2 wins currently.

The name came from South Africa and Euro = Anglo

How many stock birds do you breed from on average each season? How many babies do you produce on average?

Depending on the year I breed between 5 and 8 pairs and can breed 30-50 babies. I can fly 1 kit per day and this forces me to cull birds at times earlier then some so that my kits are not over crowded

What is the average length of time you fly a bird before using it in your stock loft?

I fly all my birds a minimum of 2 years before I try them in stock. They must spin approximately 2+ seconds to be considered as well.

What are the characteristics you look for the most with potential breeders? Can you rank the qualities of these birds in order or highest priority?

The Quality of roll is very important in the in the first 2 years. I look for birds that have good frequency and activity in the kit. Quality, Activity, Velocity, Kitting and Depth.

Here is an art rendition of a Devils Ear cock bird

Riaan's Devil Ear Rollers

You mentioned your family comes down from some birds from OD Harris birds? Are these birds related to the same birds that Hannes used in his birds? If so how are they related? Please explain the history as you know it.

Yes I mentioned this above and Hannes got started with a Ken White Red Check hen and 2 cocks from Jimmy Roodt that were out of his best cock Buks 6. It's with this cock Buks 6 that our birds are related. I also had access to many of Brian McKenzie's birds as well which are also related to Hannes' birds.

What is the best Bird you have every flown? Describe it

My best I ever bred and flew was a hen I called my "Devil-ear hen." I named my loft after this hen.

Riaan's Devil Ear "95 hen"

What has been your best stock birds in your family? What made it your best stock bird?

My "95 Hen" was the fastest pigeon I ever bred and owned in my opinion. She spun at least 1.8 seconds and her speed would destroy the feathers in her chest. She performed about twice a minute and was a perfect kitting pigeon. When she landed they were split in the middle of her chest and the ears formed on her head. This bird I would bred her and fly her every year for a 5 year period and she would always roll the same. Today my foundation cock is 332/07

What kind of schedule do you have to fly your rollers? Many of us are limited to how many birds we can keep and train due to working and or family constraints.

I run 10 km every morning at 4am and when I return I fly my young bird kit. I am only able to fly my old birds on the weekends mostly. Many guys here don't fly their old birds very often and can get them back in shape very quickly

How many kits can you manage each season? Do you have any birds of prey issues there?

I am only able to manage 2 kits each year on average; my old bird team is 4 to 5 years old and my young bird kit. All my stock birds go back out to the kit when I am done breeding from them. If I am unable to get them back up flying I will cull them. There are very few that can put their breeders back up each season after breeding from them. This is really a big thing I think with my birds that are able to breed and go back up year after year and there are very few fanciers that can do this. I think it is really frustrating to see a fancier with a hot kit and then the following year they are all gone.

Do you have any birds that you no longer fly or do you refly all your birds after breeding? Do you use foster pairs to pump out more babies from specific pairs?

I fly all my birds every season unless the bird is one that I cannot replace it with its genetics

About how many cocks and hens are in your "A" team on a normal season?

I normally don't pay attention to this so much. Many of my kits are an even split of cocks and hens. My best pigeons tend to be hens however

What advice would you give to any new flyers out there wanting to fly in competition? What is the biggest issue you see with new flyers?

I think the biggest issue I see is these new fanciers begin with too many pigeons. You need to start with high Quality birds, not a High Quantity of birds. They will find it's much easier to manage your birds. When things are easy you are able to monitor the birds easier and fly them all easier as well. It's no good to breed birds if you don't have the time to manage them properly.

I think that it will take most about 4 years before they have a good handle on their program to start competing.

You do not need a lot of birds to begin rather start with Quality than quantity ,and u find your way a lot easier breeding off les pairs and take your time, u need to work minimum 4 years with a family to start to compete. Use birds that u seen in the air, and fly a bird 2 years before you stock it.

Riaan with World Cup Finals Judge Ferrell Bussing

> IF THEY DON'T KIT, THEY DON'T SCORE. COLOUR DON'T ROLL AND PEDS DON'T FLY. IT'S A COMP THING, UNDERSTAND?
>
> THE TRUE BIRMINGHAM ROLLER TURNS OVER BACKWARDS WITH INCONCEIVABLE RAPIDITY FOR A CONSIDERABLE DISTANCE

This sign Riaan has says it all

Dr. Spintight
Question and Answer Column

This section is reserved for Q&A that are roller pigeon specific. It's my aim that this section of the magazine can assist people in moving forward in their own programs and or advancing their own knowledge of the Birmingham Roller as a high performance pigeon. It can also I help assist guys in better understanding their own birds so you are able to get the most out of them.

Interesting enough some information shared can be family lineage specific and may not work for you mostly due to not having enough data to assist you better.

If you would like to send in questions that can be answered later on please send your submissions to davesrollerpigeons@gmail.com

Hope you are able to gain some insight from the guys who submitted questions used in this issue. All names will be omitted should some think this is a dumb question, but in reality there are no dumb questions if you are needing some clarity.

Questions Submitted

#1 Do you think the birds from today are as good spinners as the ones from the past overall? By that I mean can the birds handle the roll better than in the past?

Well this is a very broad question and I hope I can narrow this for you a bit. The easy question is YES. If you interview "old timers" going back to the early 1900's about every 20 years or so that they have been active in this hobby they notice increases in overall qualities of the birds in their immediate region or area. This is not unique to say the UK or USA but to the entire world as we know it to be.

Some parts of the world might be progressing at a great rate then others but for the most part this happens to increased communication and awareness in the hobby. It's a hard "scale" to rate however because like everything the hobby evolves and the birds evolve with it. It's really a contrast that cannot be compared directly to each other due to the subjective nature of this sport/hobby.

I will answer why these aspect change over time.

If we look back around 100 years we see that the sport consisted of flying a kit of rollers and judging the birds as individuals. The birds started out much slower then we might imagine as the progression was slow and with some who had "stock sense" to breed these birds were able to achieve more in less time than others might, which this aspect is still very constant in todays' hobby as well.

In these times if a guy breed an exceptional bird it would many contests before it might vanish for whatever reason or another fancier might produce yet a better bird.

Bill Pensom was an advocate of high quality individual spinners and he was also open to learning knew things and fades as well as he progressed in own program over the years. We know this because Pensom was kicked out of the Pensom Roller Club for obtaining what are called "Competition Badges" which at this time were really just frequent tumblers.

At least in the UK these tumblers got very popular and real kit competition was developed with these "Competition Badges." As noted the birds were of relatively low quality but very frequent pigeons.

It did not take long for kit competition to come to the US where Pensom was here to really put his hands on this "baby" and educate guys on what the birds should be doing in the kit. He preached quality not quantity and because of this the US took off.

So taking this up to today and completing this question are the birds spinning better and with better control.

I would have to say yes they are. This has a lot to do with knowledge of breeding principles.

Back in Pensom's prime everyone believed that you could not pair up deep spinners to other deep spinners and must balance out the birds. This "idea" also moved on to the other facets of the birds performance to include frequency and even the quality of the spin. Everyone preached pairing frequent birds to none frequent birds or high quality spinners to the opposite to keep the balance of the birds.

As time moves on and we are better educated and actually perform our own experiments and keep records of these events we discover that all of these things as listed above were total BS. Stable birds produce stable birds no matter what depth they are and if you select birds properly you can breed anything to anything without risk of having a bunch of crap you will need to cull. I am not suggesting that unstable birds are not produced but what I am saying is that with record keeping we are able to eradicate birds that are producing unstable birds from our programs.

So yes if you are breeding and developing your line of birds correctly they will do whatever you select them to do but it doesn't happen overnight, these traits are set in our birds over a specific period of time depending on how you breed them.

I hope this answers your question.

#2 Which of the fanciers listed below have had the most lasting influence on the roller fancy and why? (Bill Pensom, Stan Plona, Ollie Harris or Bill Barrett)

I honestly wish I could answer this question without wondering if I answered it incorrectly.

As noted this is a very difficult question to answer as I had never had to pleasure of interviewing any of these guys. I could maybe rank them based on my own biases and knowledge but I can't write a simple answer to this question.

After doing extensive research on Bill Pensom in Vol 1 of Spinner Magazine (see reprint below) I would have to say the Bill Pensom would without a doubt have to be ranked #1 on this list and for good reason. Firstly Pensom was an educator to the populous for all of us life on the Birmingham Roller. He wrote more article to better educate fanciers then probably anyone living today has. Now was he correct on all these things? Well of course not as I have constantly preached that everyone who pays attention and aims to create the best possible rollers they can are always learning about these rollers of ours and part of this is brain storming ideas to others. This sort of things gives us clarity. So I think Pensom would be #1 on this just for the simple fact that his ideals on the quality of the True Birmingham Roller still plays on today and these things are still discussed even after Pensom died in 1968 and this has to say something.

Pensom had to have been a real flyer or they would not have named a competition in England after him, Pensom Sheild. So this leads me to think they were aware of his abilities as well. His fame was really brought to life in the United States as when he moved here this was all new territory for him, very exciting times I bet, and he could do what he does best by educating others and he didn't miss a beat when he got here in or around 1950.

I think the difference for the most part was that due to his Pensom Imports he was very well recognized here in the US and he really stepped into a perfect role here. Now if the question had to do with who had the best birds or flew the best kits the answer could be different but again this is only because the UK was farther advanced in this evolution of the Birmingham Roller at the time they become popular here in the United States. I mean the breed is for one called the Birmingham Roller, meaning Birmingham, England.

I know if you look at the guys that are doing the best with the Birmingham Rollers in competition today you will find that Heine Bijker of the Netherlands who is said to have a line of birds that are primarily Barrett based birds. I know nothing about their background really but this is what I have been told. They claim that Barrett's kits had a very slow butterfly action to them and that Bijker's kits also have this which they say confirms this. How close or how much Barrett blood are in these birds I have no idea, but Heine has won the World Cup 4 times and does so on an average of every 5 years or so. This could give us some idea of how influential Barrett's birds could have been over the years. Barrett spoke highly of Pensom and even had a few birds in his loft in the early years that came from Pensom so Barrett's were part Pensom right?

If we dig dipper we find that Bob Brown was the most decorated roller kit flyer in England and he flew Barrett birds also. Some might say he had them long enough to create his own and no doubt he did but upon further research Bob Brown only got birds from Barrett and over the years got birds on average of every 3-5 years from Barrett. So to me this meant he relied heavily on Barrett for the birds that caused "Hybrd Vigor" in his which tend to be very good for competition, even if of the same lineage. **(As noted in the article earlier in this issue about "Pretzel Breeding")** So they say Barrett might not have been such a great flyer but he was a fantastic breeder of high quality rollers.

I think possibly the best on this list could be Ollie Harris, however he was not well versed in writing but was known for his very good deep high velocity spinners. Ollie was also a 3rd generation roller flyer so we know he learned his skills at an early age on how to be successful in breeding high quality birds. Having been a 3rd generation breeder/flyer takes Ollie and his family almost back to the inception of the Birmingham Roller when it was named as such.

There are many today that are flying some of the best high quality birds that are said to have strong ties to OD Harris blood in them and others that claim they are still flying birds they got directly from Ollie. The Harris birds are in fact a very popular blood to have in birds these days and we see this in the US as well as in South Africa.

If we take it back a notch we find that Bill Pensom used to go back to England every couple years after moving to California and would bring back multiple birds on each trip. I am uncertain as to what or why on this birds but I would imagine it was part of why he went back to the UK to scout more bird to bring here for other fanciers. So by doing this it was almost like a "business" trip for him. However in 1965 he made one last trip to England I heard and brought back approximately 14 pigeons from OD Harris that were for him personally. It was said they were some of the best birds he had possession of and some that could assist him in his own program. So in this simple thing it seems that Pensom thought very highly of Ollie Harris and his birds as well. So this is kind of where I bring to the conclusion that possibly Ollie Harris might be the most influential fancier on this list even though we don't see a lot of literature about him.

I cannot really comment on Stan Plona although I have heard is was a very capable kit flyer. I have seen some birds that were descendants of his line thru Tom Hatcher back in the 1980's and they were mere tumblers in my view. A lady I know who also got some from his family also from Tom and she had some exceptional spinners but the one major negative was they would become roll downs within 7-8 months of age. I found it odd how the ones I got would totally opposite to hers, in fact total opposites.

The biggest void in the background of the Birmingham Roller is that there is really no written information that takes us much further back then around 1870's so we have no real idea of what combination of birds created the Birmingham Roller. They do have DNA today and with DNA you can see the percentages of the various breeds in there that created the BR, but not really sure it will tell us that much as different strains would have been developed slightly different and which is which we can only speculate.

****There is an interesting facet in comparison to the UK and US and this is that the vast majority flying birds in the UK have a lot of white on their birds and many here in the US have a lot more self-colored birds. I have thought about his phenomenon a bit and I think it could be the type of weather they have in comparison ours especially in California. I see more self colored birds in South Africa also and they also have a lot of sunny days there. What I mean by this is that in areas where you get a lot of sun you can see all colors equally but in an area that is heavily overcast, like the UK, self-colored birds are very difficult to tell apart while flying. So I think you might get where I am going with this. This is just an idea I have.

I wish I could write more about this but there is just no real data to confirm much. Many in the UK were not able to read and write well but they were not dumb, just illiterate. At the same time in the US many more were able to better communicate like Pensom did. There is also a slight language issue from the US and the UK with meaning to words which plays into a lot of this.

The interesting thing with competition is standards will evolve just like the BR does in some places. If I could go back and interview all 4 of these guys and also see their kits in action based on what I know now I could compile a great deal more on this topic but I obviously can't.

I would like to thank Eric Laidler who has an extensive library of old literature and he has greatly helped me to learn more about the background of the BR in the UK in the early days.

Hope this might help you to understand a little more about it but it's obviously not going to be the kind of information that will "blow up your skirt" so to speak.

#3 Do white flights on birds play a major role in the birds performance and in your long term breeding program?

Again with rollers color means very little in the development of a line or family of rollers. These things are personal preferences or just what the birds were that you developed them from. I really don't see any real links, personally to specific colors.

Unlike the balancing of the qualities that birds have there are things that lead us to believe that we should be color balancing our birds.

There are basically 2 colors that dominate in the Birmingham Roller, not taking into account any white on the birds, and that is blue check and ash red check. Of course there are many modifiers that will make birds look differently in appearance even if genetically they are simply a blue check or ash red check.

We need to learn how to breed our specific family of rollers and get the most out of them. This has much more to do with management and not so much on color. This would involve feeding and flying them.

A major issue for some is not culling enough or hard enough. We need to have high standards if we hope to fly world class kits in competitions like the World Cup Fly.

So the basic answer is that what you ask has more to do with a specific line or family of birds than it does to the breed as a whole.

#4 To what degree does body type affect the roll/spin? Should we be breeding for long/short or sharp keel?

Well to be honest body type has everything to do with the quality and how the birds spin. However there are exceptions to nearly every scenario there is in regard to this.

As we look and analyze our best and fastest birds in our own family of birds we can see things that are specific to families however in many cases of my personally seeing the best fast and best quality spinners I have noticed many things over the years.

One thing I have to say is that feather is a major player in rolling ability. This means having TOO much feather or feathers that are too thick and big.

Just like many things that fly these things create "drag" and with airplanes there are specific designs that are faster planes then others. Granted this can also be affected on how big the engine is. So bigger engines can generate more speed.

However looking back at mother nature things are not quite like they are with aerodynamics we use with aircraft flown by humans.

Again preference will play a major part in this in terms of body type. Many areas are unable to fly birds all year long and these areas might also be very cold and due to these areas the birds change slightly in type over time.

The thing you will notice is the birds tend to gravitate to the larger side and birds that are able to keep on body weight better. This is just simple survival 101 as it was in caveman days.

The other thing that plays into these areas is a long period of locking down the birds due to heavy BOP issues or just super cold conditions where the birds are needing to eat so much food that it will hinder their ability to fly and perform like they are capable of doing, so guys instead will start showing their birds more often than not and this desire to do well in these shows also changes their "flavor" of birds they breed.

It's been my own experience that the birds that are slim in the body but still solid feeling are the best spinners, the fastest spinners.

Carolina Performing Roller Club
Representing Region 1D

Members
Cliff Ball - Jay Yandle - Dennis Cook
Van Newsome - Greg Wilkerson - Greg Truesdale

more info contact
Dennis - 704-791-7116 - cccsoftball247@aol.com

Health Tip

Always wear a mask when scraping loft

Southern Gauteng Region
consists of five clubs in South Africa

V.R.K - Vanderbijlpark Roller Club Albert Wallis, Wynand Deyzel, Charles Puth, Hennie De Bruyn, Hennie Phal, Hannes Rossouw	**G.B.R.C - Gold Reef Birmingham Roller Club** Niekie Deysel, Jan Deysel, Rob Lombaard, Jan Lubbe, Johan Venter
S.A.B.R.C - South African Birmingham Roller Club Poen Sahabodien, Willem Potgieter, Mark Sacks, Walter Benfield, Riaan Naude	**H.P.S - Hyper Paints Spinners** Dominic Peter, John Paul Peter, Mark Peter, Jade Peter, Gesham Thebe, John Chauke

W.R.K - WestRand Roller Club
Sparks Axsel, Dirk Axsel, Tommy Laubscher, Christo Troskie, Theo Troskie, Basie Masiso, Henk van der Westhuizen

Regional Director - Niekie Deysel
Ndeysel@deyco.co.za

The Pensom Legend
By
Dave Henderson

Here Trophy in hand Bill Pensom, from Google Images

Bill Pensom was born in 1904 and passed away in 1968 and resided in the US for his last 18 years of his life. Pensom was a 3rd generation roller fanciers same as Ollie Harris, which appears was common in the Black Country with generations of pigeon breeders in the old days.

I of course never got to meet Bill Pensom but none the less here on the West Coast of the United States he was legendary for his birds and knowledge, after nearly 50 years since he has passed there are many that still make reference to Pensom Rollers out here, especially from the Kiser/Borges birds which are very prevalent in this region. If you look at things closer in fact most of the birds on the West Coast go back to Pensom Imports and many of the birds of today still have this same blood running thru them, this is for the most part also the same blood that the UK fanciers today are flying, but for various reasons each side has bred them for their own characteristics over the years. Laron Doucet says that many of the high velocity spinners all trace back to long ago fancier named Harry Young.

Pensom came to the US with a lifetime of knowledge and experience to a region that was eager to learn and he became our teacher. Southern California has been a very rich roller hot bed of history for the flying Birmingham Roller, in a large part due to Bill Pensom relocating there. Quality spinners has remained consistent in Southern California over the years and this has spread Worldwide now. Not that Pensom was the inventor or creator of the Birmingham Roller but that he brought a degree awareness to those that listened and read his "how to" articles about the True Birmingham Roller. Just like breeding the Birmingham Roller today it will not come easy and those that will benefit the most will pay great attention to the qualities and characteristics of these fascinating pigeons and breed/fly your rollers with a scientific approach.

After talking to some and reading about Bill Pensom's influence in the UK, he appears to have been a pretty average well respected roller fancier in the UK, but nowhere near the Legend that he was here in the US. It could have been that Pensom was somehow being held down by his peers in the UK and/or due to respect to the hobby over there or he just did not take his game up a notch until he was placed into a full time **"teaching"** and authority position with the Birmingham Rollers like here in the US. These are things I really wish I could ask Pensom himself.

It was obvious that Pensom was at a level with the birds like no other in his generation here and it is with jealousy that some belittle what Bill Pensom achieved in his tenure. I think Pensom was not unlike many others that can build a solid foundation of managing the birds at every degree; from selection, breeding and flying the Birmingham Roller in a manner as to increase your awareness and understanding of these pigeons. Many just don't really pay close enough attention to the birds to learn more about them.

Pensom obviously did fly competition in the UK as the picture above shows him holding a fly trophy. The All England Roller Club also has a competition called the **"Pensom Shield"** that started in 1966, this would not be in place had Pensom not been who he was. The late great Bill Barrett had a lot of good things to say about Pensom and he claims he promoted the rollers in the UK and educated fanciers in how to breed more good rollers and manage their own birds. He did this in part with articles he wrote as well as speaking to fanciers that had little knowledge of how to breed and get the most performance out of their rollers and it appears he did the same thing here in the US.

To my recollection Bill Pensom was brought to the US by a handful of well to do roller fanciers with goals of further educating themselves on how to breed and fly the True Birmingham Roller first hand, which in turn got everyone familiar with what top quality roll was, especially here in California. By the time Pensom came to the US kit competition was a big thing in the UK and Pensom was more in the mindset of the Individual high quality spinners at the time and foresaw kit competition ruining the True Birmingham Rollers as he saw it. I have been told that eventually Pensom got some competition rollers from his close friend Ken Payne and was consequently pushed out of the Pensom Roller Club (he resigned) for doing so and this brought on the creation of the National Birmingham Roller Club that is still in existence today.

Pensom had been a carpenter for many years, he knew how to build lofts and I have heard he was working for Andrew's Hardware in Southern California. Pensom was essentially Don Andrew's loft manager. Andrew's was instrumental in creating the Pageant of Pigeons in Southern California. Andrew's also had a ton of pigeon supplies in those days. Pensom I think was semi-retired and even published his roller book in 1958, 8 years after moving in the US, **The Birmingham Roller Pigeon**.

I had not picked up this book since the late 1980's and as I recall back then that many were preaching it as the "Holy Bible" of the Birmingham Roller. I actually preferred True Spinners by David Kowalski much more but I was really not in the "Pensom Generation". I think True Spinners was easier to read and there really was not a lot of "know how" books on rollers when I was growing up except for articles in publications like the American Pigeon Journal, which published a load of articles by Bill Pensom.

Here is probably the most famous bird Pensom owned, #514 PRC 1953 hen. Pensom did not discover her worth until she was about 5 years old, which tells me his selection system was not perfect or he would have discovered her sooner. Both parents as I recall were bred by JL Smith and not Pensom

After many years I recently picked up Pensom's book again, with 30 years of experience under my belt, I can tell in this book that Bill Pensom knew what he was doing and I have no hesitations that he knew what a first rate spinner was and how to breed them. I could also tell that a high quality spin was his passion. Pensom spent many hours researching characteristics of the True Birmingham Roller to find out why it was like it was. He paid attention to the small details and was even said to have the ability to select top quality breeders on the ground thru physical characteristics. They talk about Bill Richards having this same ability so I would assume that Richards might even have showed this to Bill Pensom in his youth, Pensom was only a young man when Richards died.

I suspect that much of the characteristics he paid attention to was the eye of the roller and other subtle physical qualities that birds have.   It could've been "eye clusters" even but can't recall any mention to this by Pensom? We just know he would look at the eye of the pigeons in his selection process.

The main flying quality that Pensom bred for and preached was the "H" style spinners when I was first getting into flying rollers, at least many were telling me that this was his preferred style. I am uncertain how good Pensom's eye sight was but I think after the late 1970's everyone came to the conclusion that "H" style was not the preferred style and something more like what I call an "A" style or small spinning ball was preferred but very rare. I think many will simply say they like the wings to be in an upward position while spinning and I would agree with this, but in reality the wings are however in a downward position as we know now, it's just the bird is upside down when we see the "H" or "A" style. I discuss more of this in my own book.

LaRon Doucet talks about a **"Pensom Strain"** of the Birmingham Roller back in the UK that many were not aware of. I really can't say he didn't have a Pensom Strain here in the US as he did live here for 18 years which is plenty of time to create such a strain but after speaking to several in the UK region it seemed that Pensom was continually picking up good quality birds all the time in the Black Country from various sources, this was not uncommon in the old days. What I have seen however is that he was not just content with the birds in his loft and was still continuing to get birds from Smith and Plona while in the US as well as many others. It is said that Pensom parked some of his prized rollers at various loft so as to shield himself from would be thieves. He also imported some other birds from Ollie Harris for himself in 1965, I assume some of these had to have gone to Herb Sparkes as these are the birds that Joe Kiser and Joe Borges have had for many years now. Technically this were not "Pensom Rollers" but instead Harris birds that Pensom imported. I would have to say from what I have seen and heard that Pensom was somewhat of a collector here in the US and as well as in the UK, old habits are hard to break. Chan Grover was also a collector for as long as I knew him, so this could be a generational thing. This does not mean that Pensom did not possess top quality rollers but it puts a big question mark (?) on this "Pensom Strain" that LaRon speaks about.

There is no secret that people that are successful with performance rollers tend to keep to a small gene pool and seldom bring in stray birds from other lofts, in the UK we saw this with both Skidmore and Richards. So with the tendency to do what Pensom was doing leads me to believe that there really was not a **"REAL"** Pensom Strain like he talks about but more of a collection of Pensom birds that were worthy of what he deemed a True Birmingham Roller.

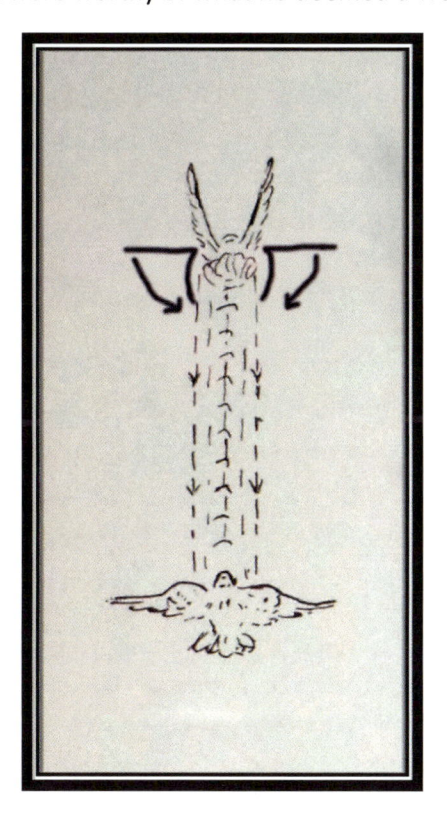

In the diagram you see what Pensom believed back in 1958 but in reality the roller does a series of ½ downward strokes and the wings really never raise above the back, the downward thrusts is what pushes the roller into a series of (revolution) of backwards somersaults

Even in the article in this booklet by Bill Pensom called **"Breeding the Birmingham Roller Pigeon"** he himself makes note of the different strains and families he imported, noting they were not the same pigeons, even though they all became known here in the US as "Pensom Rollers". I think it just goes on to tell you that you can get good spinners as long as you select for it no matter what the blood lines are, so long as the birds mix well together, this is found out through good ole "trial and error".

What really made a Pensom Roller the Pensom Rollers people have been talking about all these years? To me it appears obvious that they were called Pensom Roller due to him importing rollers to the US from the UK. This is because everyone knows that all the birds that were imported to the US were not bred by Pensom. Had they all been bred by Pensom I think I would be more adapt to calling them Pensom's, but this is not the case. Pensom imported literally hundreds of rollers to the US from the UK. He sent 44 birds alone in the mid 1930's.

The Kiser/Borges birds that are also called Pensom's were in fact birds in part from Ollie Harris in the Pensom Imports. I was told this by many out there to include the late Chan Grover. This was why Kiser/Borges did their own importation from Ollie Harris in 1981. So why do people still call these birds in the #272 line Pensom Rollers if the genetic background is from Ollie Harris? This really does not compute to me. Even Ollie himself stated in his 1987 interview that if he were to get any birds to bring back into his family it would be birds from Sparkes here in the US. So Ollie obviously felt very strongly about the birds he had sent in 1965 to the US.

I suppose it all goes back to marketing the birds? Pensom was a name or a brand and this gave fanciers a better ability to market the bird for sale maybe? I would say this makes more sense than anything else. Pensom states he did not like to give out pedigrees on his birds, for the fear that people could manufacture a pedigree and sell it as a "Pensom Roller" no matter what kind of bird it was. He would mostly just give the parents of the said bird as he felt the other birds on that list would mean nothing to the fancier getting the rollers from him.

I have seen some minor changes to this in recent years where some are calling these old Kiser/Borges birds now Harris birds, which might be more acceptable, but all the same they have been in the US no less than 33 years now these should not have any mention to Pensom or Harris at this time. They should have taken on their own strain by whomever is working with them right? I think this again is a marketing ploy as we see a lot of popularity in the UK birds here in the US in recent years mostly from George Mason birds, but the list also includes Stratford, McKinney (Ireland), Bijker (Holland) and even South Africa birds from Hannes Rassouw down from the late Ron Swart. Again I see this more as a marketing scheme as since 2009 the US has been getting beat by many of the other countries to include the; UK, Ireland, South Africa, Australia just to name a few.

In the UK Pensom knew there was a huge market in the US for the Birmingham Roller and many of the UK fanciers breeding these birds were more than willing to sell their top birds for cash to help support their family and Pensom Imports to the US started in 1932 when Pensom was only 28 years old. I would suspect that the early shipments in 1932 and 1936 might have had the many of them bred by Pensom but I am not aware of this in the exact numbers. The later shipments to Smith and Plona were the birds Pensom was more interested I have heard.

I am not sure what a good roller was worth in the 1930 thru 1960's in the US but they might have been worth more to US fanciers than to the UK counterparts and this was why the importations continued I am sure. Barrett said he had 1 pigeon (best birds from a particular fanciers loft) in his foundation which cost him 12 Shillings, which in today's prices would be approximately $18 US dollars, he said that $18 was nearly a week's wages in 1947 in the Black Country. By today's standards you are not going to get the best bird from a guy's loft for $18, it's not going to happen. This is not much of a comparison to the $50 or more that fanciers will pay today's market, in fact many will pay hundreds of dollars for specific pigeons. So I think this was the main driving force for the UK fanciers to sell off their prized rollers to the Americans.

However after talking to Donny of Ireland he confirms that over time as Pensom continued to ask for more and more birds to ship to America, the guys started holding back their prized stock. So what he told me was that the first couple of shipments were top rate but as the shipments continued to come the quality of the birds in the shipments decreased substantially. They were no longer going to part with their best pigeons but Pensom still had orders to fill and to ship to America. I think you can get the jest of the story here.

The Pensom imports worked two fold for Pensom. Firstly he was making good money for the fanciers who would normally get very little money for their top pigeons and secondly he was getting access to these birds for personal use as well. Birds that he had access too he might not have had the money to purchase them personally but becoming a **"Roller Broker"** gave him the ability to get access to these fine pigeons. I call him a broker as he imported Birmingham Rollers from the top lofts in the Black Country, somewhere between 10-20 strains in fact. The fanciers bred birds for high velocity quality spinning and the majority of them were from 15-30 feet deep.

Here are the original "Pensom Imports" from 1932, Pensom was only 28 years old at the time, to Father Schlattmann of St Louis.

HRC 32.18 Blue Self Hen
HRC 32.5 Clay Hen
HRC 32.195 Blue Check Oddity Hen
HRC 32.166 Black Badge Cock
HRC 31.1 Blue Badge Cock
HRC 30.464 White Black Neck Cock
HRC 30.885 Blue Saddle Cock
HRC 27.1007 Black Bald Cock

Other importers followed to include; J. Leroy Smith of New York; Raymond Perkins of Connecticut, Chandler Grover of New Jersey, Ciro Valenti of Missouri, Al Walker of Michigan and Francis Buckley also of New York. The majority of the birds came from Pensom or Jim Skidmore, however there were up to as many as twenty different lofts in these imports, many strains of families. These all would go on to become "Pensom Rollers". Bill Pensom imported in his last pigeons in 1965 and I read they all came from Ollie Harris. I was told this last importation was for Pensom himself.

In the original imports, it appears that 4 of these birds were in fact young birds when Pensom shipped them (3 of them young hens) and one was no doubt right out of Pensom stock loft being a 1927 bird. What does this tell us? Well it doesn't tell us much really, but what Father Schlattmann did with them is the real story he did share his pigeons with others and help started the craze of Pensom Imports as the velocity in which these "Pensom" rollers performed was a drastic improvement over the Whittingham Rollers at the same time. There was a lot of unknowns to what happened to Father Schlattmann but was said to have died in a auto accident in the 1940's and where the birds ended up I am not sure. I would hope that they ended up in a loft so that they could continue to be improved upon. It would be interesting if someone had pedigrees going back to these original imports in their lofts, but then again how could you insure this over several generations of roller breeders. This is was the stuff that Pensom was warning us of, there is a lot of greed out there.

As Barrett openly admits his family of pigeons had a great deal of Pensom behind them, more than any other line, but they did not continue to be called "Pensom's" they became Barrett Birds. As does many fine lines of rollers even today. They all started from a fairly small gene pools and then thru selective breeding and a great deal of diligence they came up with a very steady and reliable family of spinners. There reaches a point where the person breeding and flying them needs to take credit for what they have done; good or bad. If your aim is to sell birds for top dollar then your only option is to join the mainstream and compete with the best of them. This is really the only way you will be able to get $100 or more per bird if that is your intention, at least long term. The roller hobby is a friendly one for the most part and money is generally not a main concern for most, it's bettering the hobby as a whole and this approach gives longevity to our hobby. Granted giving all your birds away will not help either, as many won't have "worth" in them and could waste them easier if not handled correctly.

I think ultimately Pensom greatly enjoyed and wanted to help other fanciers become successful like many others in the hobby do even today, but he certainly could not afford to give every bird away just because someone wanted them. Bill Pensom was just a normal guy like many of us but he took it upon himself to create more for this hobby. He wanted to promote and educate fanciers to get the most out of their own pigeons to better the hobby in general, this type of thing takes a lot of volunteer work of writing articles and giving advice to get there.

Over the years you see and read interviews with well-known fanciers too and many of them are asked, "Are the birds better today than they were 20 years ago?" I have not seen one individual in modern times, after Pensom, state the birds are now worse than they were over the past 20 years. This has everything to do with communication within the hobby and fanciers understanding what needs to be done to breed and fly the best birds we can. It's with a sound breeding system and good record keeping practices.

There may never been the number of fanciers there once was back in the Black Country during the 1920's and 1930's but the fanciers that are still doing it today are far better educated and able to do more with them. Competition never did ruin the Birmingham Roller and I think Pensom would be very proud to see what kit competition has evolved to with our modern World Cup Fly.

Thanks to the sources that were made available to me on this topic, more than I can name here.

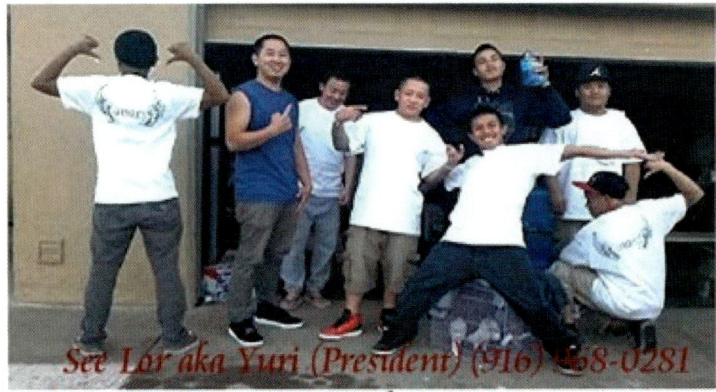

HMONG BIRMINGHAM ROLLER CLUB

See Lor aka Yuri (President) (916) 868-0281

Members
Sor Lor - Koua Vang - Teng Lor - Pao Vue - CJ Vang - Johnny Her
FOLLOW US ON FACEBOOK

SPEED - DEPTH - VELOCITY - RESPECT - FAMILY - SACRAMENTO

Planning and Patience → Success

I want to thank Vince for sitting down and contributing to this issue of Spinner Magazine. I have only known Vince for about 18 months now but he is well on his way to implementing a solid plan to a successful program. Nothing happens overnight and if you willing to plan and put the time in to be successful then you will eventually get there and learn a lot. It's been a real pleasure having someone that I can brain storm with again about something I am so passionate about.

The Plan
By
Vince van Royen

Dave Henderson asked me if I would write an article for Spinner Magazine about my plan. So here is my article by request.

Given that there are only about a bazillion different things to write about when it comes to Rollers, I decided to touch on just a few.

First off, let's look at the difference between building a family of first class performers vs. building a collection of Rollers that have very little in common, other than that they can fly and roll in a sloppy, unpredictable manner. Of the two, building a collection is the easiest thing in the world to do. Make the rounds and get free or cheap Rollers from as many people as possible. In no time at all, you can pronounce yourself a Roller guy/gal and begin opinionating on as many online roller sites as you care to visit. Now, if this works for you, by all means go for it. For some of us though, we prefer to take the longer, much harder, but in the end the most satisfying path to our own definition of success.

Vince main loft

Since I can't speak for other people, or their personal methods of building a family of high-quality Rollers, I'll write about my own plan/plans.

Having been in pigeons and birds for almost 50 years, I've learned that there are many, many different aspects to success, no matter what the breed. The time-honored first step is always the same; have a plan. Secondly, make every possible effort to get the best stock that you can find to put that plan into action. It's always better to buy your birds and own them outright, than it is to have a loft full of Rollers that belong to other people. The drama that can occur when something happens to a "loaner" bird can get real ugly, real quick. If you are offered a bird, (or birds) make sure you discuss up front your level of responsibility in case of a loss (or losses). In addition, make sure that you know how long you can use the bird/birds and return them as soon as that time period is up. Tread carefully here; many friendships have ended in an ugly way when someone's request for the return of a top bird is ignored, or worse yet, the bird (and the person who has the bird) simply vanishes without a trace.

I have been blessed with generous, knowledgeable friends who have helped me with my plan by putting birds in my hands that will be the foundation birds for my family. After studying a lot of birds, kits, and the loft management of many different people, my choices came down to a combination of birds from Gene Varao's family of Harris/Hiltons, Dave Henderson's family for their superb kitting, and Robert Rives birds that fly almost every day including the 100+ degree summer days that we get in this area. I have always felt that you need to have birds that are suited to the area that you plan to fly in. Weak birds have no place in either the breeder loft or the kit box.

Since this article can't begin to cover the whole spectrum of Roller breeding and flying, I'm going to lay out some of the things that I want to accomplish as far as building my own family, based on my likes and dislikes. Everyone will have their own vision, as far as type of performance, body style, wing action, and whether they plan to fly in competition or just for personal enjoyment. First and foremost, I have to please myself and no one else. If you constantly chop and change your program based on too much input from too many people, you will' never see the same results that you would from a well-executed plan consisting of both short-term and long-term goals.

One of the key factors of success with Rollers is the constant studying of your birds as often as possible, from the day they hatch to the time that they make the grade in the air, and then into the breeding loft. No studying, no true success. So in a nutshell, here's what I want from my birds, and while everyone will see things differently, this is what I want.

From day one I want to see babies that are determined to survive whatever hardships come their way, combined with an above average intelligence that will enable them to respond to my training methods without going "dummy up" on me. Next up is the desire to take to the air without having to be flagged up or chased off roofs, power lines, and trees, and homing ability. Any young bird that can't figure out how to get home even on a clear, BOP-free day, can stay gone. I have no problem with the ones that come back in a day or two after a BOP attack, or a sudden change in weather conditions etc.

Remember what I said about intelligence and survival instinct? The two should go hand in hand with each other in a top quality Roller, without exception. Speaking only for myself, I prefer strong, powerful flyers that come into their spin after they've developed their air skills. And yes, I said spin, not roll. I want speed, velocity, and control in my birds. I also want a deeper bird with phenomenal kitting ability. Out birds that can't or won't kit are guaranteed to cause more problems than they're worth.

When it comes to trapping, my mantra is "In it in a minute". No sitting around, no flying down to the ground and wandering around like a commie. These birds are supposed to be athletes, so I pursue a simple formula when it comes to release and return time... it goes like this. Out, up, fly, down, and in. Birds that don't follow that program are prime targets (In this area) for Cooper hawk attacks. I have no intention of creating a BOP fly-through fast food snack bar, and birds that won't trap are like the crazy relative that won't go home, and causes nothing but problems for you.

In the interest of keeping this article shorter, rather than longer, if Dave wants me to go into more detail in the future I'll do so.

For now, best wishes to everyone in 2018, and remember that these birds are athletes, and you're the whole management team from coach to water boy.

Some of Vince's 2018 young birds

OUTLAW ROLLER CLUB

For more Info
Tim Paustian
timothypaustian@gmail.com

Southwestern Los Angeles

MRPC — Midland Roller Pigeon Club

Ted Mann

As I am pushed to write this last minute update for this issue of Spinner Magazine it comes with a heavy heart when another roller friend has passed away.

In Volume 2 the subheading on the cover read; *"Ted Mann brings World Cup title back to US"*. I was lucky enough to have had a connection to Ted that dates back to 1995 here in Redding where I live and Ted is from the Redding area originally and went to the same high school I did actually. I was unsure if it was the same Ted until I asked him as it had been 19 years since I last saw him. He openly gave me an interview for Spinner Magazine shortly after he won the cup. It was very exciting times for everyone involved and Ted was gracious enough to share some of his prized birds with many on the west coast since then.

I got a call in the evening of March 16th, 2018 from my old friend Ivan Hanchett of Oregon. Ivan called and asked if I had heard that Ted had passed away and at that point heard nothing about it. He said that Ted's friend Bruce would be handling the birds and gave me his number.

It's tuff to find the right words to tell others what Ted meant to me as a friend over the last 3 years now and it always great hearing from Ted and his progress. I used to randomly get these long texts late at night from Ted of his ideas about the birds and his program as Ted was very involved in making the birds better. He was like most of us and still learning the birds he has and how to maximize their performance. He gave a lot of credit to Ron Swart when he won the World Cup in 2015 and was refining his methods.

This year I think Ted had his sights on a repeat and I had heard a lot of good things about the birds he was flying bred from 2017. He sent me a message not even 2 months ago saying that him and Bruce were in the back yard watching the birds fly and they were doing some great things, breaking together in huge clusters at depth of 40-50 foot range. I am going to post a few of Ted's favorite birds and we have for sure lost a good one.

Ted was only 67 and retired not long before he won the World Cup. I know Ted is up there somewhere flying amongst the others we have lost over the years. He will truly be missed in my life and many others. Rest in Peace my friend.

02 and 063 hens, 062 on cover

Ted's infamous 21 cock bird

Printed in Great Britain
by Amazon